AF173655

More Ghost Walks
in Derbyshire

More Ghost Walks
in Derbyshire

by

Barbara Wadd

DB
PUBLISHING

First published in Great Britain in 2007 by
The Breedon Books Publishing Company Limited
Breedon House, 3 The Parker Centre,
Derby, DE21 4SZ.

This edition published in Great Britain in 2012 by The Derby Books Publishing
Company Limited, 3 The Parker Centre, Derby, DE21 4SZ.

© Barbara Wadd, 2007

All Rights Reserved. No part of this publication may be reproduced,
stored in a retrieval system, or transmitted in any form, or by any means,
electronic, mechanical, photocopying, recording or otherwise without the prior
permission in writing of the copyright holders, nor be otherwise circulated in
any form or binding or cover other than in which it is published and without a
similar condition being imposed on the subsequent publisher.

ISBN 978-1-78091-178-6

Printed and bound by Copytech (UK) Limited, Peterborough.

Index of Walks

Acknowledgements

I wish to acknowledge the contribution made to this book by my friends Susan Broadrick and Pete Wallace.

Pete, you took on the role of chief 'walk checker' this time around and did it thoroughly, efficiently and sometimes psychically, managing to realise that when I said right I really meant left! You did a superb job, and I could not have done it without you.

And my special friend Sue: after walking 400 miles with me on the first book, you enthusiastically and amazingly supported the idea of a second. You checked my map reading, got lost with me, retraced steps over many miles without complaining and then did each walk over again, while Pete checked them.

Most of all, you made it all so enjoyable, cheerfully wading through mud more suited to a hippopotamus and laughing as we hacked our way through nettles that could have done with a machete.

I couldn't have had a better companion and co-writer.

Introduction

This is a second collection of 30 circular walks set in Derbyshire and the Peak District, the walks ranging from 1 to 10 miles in length. Each walk has at least one ghostly story attached to a part of it, some walks having several chilling tales, which, hopefully, will make a rambler shiver even under the warmest fleece! The stories include bridges where you may encounter headless phantoms or ghostly troops of soldiers, faceless horsemen, a plethora of monks and a bespectacled nun, famous ghosts haunting halls and houses and, one you won't want to meet, a man-eating family!

Many of the ghosts are active, making their presence felt by turning on taps, switching on lights, moving camcorders and, in one case, burning down premises.

And you should be warned that some of the ghosts are more 'hands on', so you may be pinched or pushed, slapped or have your clothes tugged. You may be locked in a room or shut in a freezer and you may even receive three cold kisses!

The walks cover a wide range of Derbyshire scenery and visit some of the less frequented parts where you will be unlikely to see another walker. You will experience the rich diversity of the countryside, enjoying the delights of fields, woods and valleys, rivers, lakes and reservoirs, climb gentle hills and visit panoramic viewpoints.

On these quieter paths, you will find wildlife undisturbed by the tramp of many feet. Kestrels hover over pastures, jays and woodpeckers may be glimpsed in woodland, buntings chirp from uncut hedges, and, if you are lucky, on three of the walks a kingfisher may imprint its brilliant hue on your day.

As well as the ghostly tales, some of the walks include visits to famous halls, houses and castles and the chance to see a number of fascinating churches, ranging from one of the smallest in England (25ft by 26ft) to the strangely named Halter Devil Chapel and one where the Devil dictated where it should be built, by continually removing the stones overnight from its original site. In addition, there is information on unusual features like a Holy Well, Seven Spouts Farm and a Hangman's Stone, along with explanations of strange place names and some unusual folktales and legends.

Each walk has an introductory description telling you the area covered, the type of terrain and highlighting its best attributes. Your attention is drawn to special features, such as a recommended time of year for doing the walk, for example, late spring because the woods are full of bluebells and wild garlic.

The distance of each walk is given in miles and the walks are graded from A to C, i.e. from easy to energetic, with an explanation of the grades being provided at the front of the book.

Information is given regarding parking at the start of the walk, together with directions where necessary. A map grid reference is also stated.

Details of where refreshments may be obtained and WC facilities are identified where available, both at the start of walks and en route.

My friends and I have walked over 400 miles to put these walks together, compiling the routes and checking that the instructions are correct and as unambiguous as possible. Therefore, the walk directions are very detailed and, hopefully, clear, and the text has been broken into numbered sections that relate to a sketch map. The sketch map also shows features such as farms, woods, roads and other points, which should assist you in navigation.

'Confirmers', i.e. points that tell you that you are on the right path, are included throughout the instructions, and some, such as the name of a lane or farm, may be checked against an Ordnance Survey map if carried.

If the instructions do not seem to match the terrain, stop and think for a moment. If necessary, retrace your steps to the last point where they fitted, rather than continuing and trying to make them fit.

A map is not essential for the walks, but information is given as to which Ordnance Survey map may be used. You may find one useful as an aid to navigation or in case you have to divert from the planned route due to, for example, flooding. It is also an easy way to get used to map reading, by checking the walk instructions against a map and seeing how the information fits.

It has been my intention to produce a book which will be useful and interesting, intriguing and amusing, and one which, while showing you the delights of the Derbyshire countryside, will also give you a taste of its rich folk history.

I hope that you will enjoy using it as much as I have enjoyed compiling it.

Degree of Difficulty

The walks are graded as follows, taking into account ascents, descents, terrain underfoot and length of walks. Grading may span two categories.

A. Easy: Gently undulating terrain. Taking into account the mileage, it should be well within the capabilities of regular walkers and fit occasional walkers.

B. Moderate: One or two longer or steeper ascents/descents but suitable for regular walkers who can manage the distance.

C. Energetic: Steeper ascents/descents, distance and rougher terrain making it a more demanding walk. Should be within the capabilities of reasonably experienced regular walkers.

Equipment:
Walking boots are recommended for all the walks. In view of the mileage, they will make even the walks graded A more enjoyable. In dry summer weather, lightweight boots would be suitable for A and B grades.
Suitable outerwear, including waterproof coats and trousers, hats and gloves should be taken.

Other equipment recommended:
Food and drink: At least some emergency rations, e.g. chocolate for a quick energy boost. Also take plenty of water in summer to avoid dehydration and a hot drink in winter.
Compass: An essential piece of equipment for any walker.
Whistle: For emergency use only.

Torch (and spare batteries): In case you misjudge the time and night falls.
Survival Bag or Space Blanket: Useful in case of accident to wrap casualty
to keep them warm.
Rucksack: Leaves hands free.
First Aid kit: Plasters, blister kit and antiseptic cream.
Maps: Not essential as detailed instructions and a sketch map are provided.
However, a map is useful as a back-up in case of confusion or in the event
of diversion from the walk route due to adverse conditions.

Other Terms used in text:
Green Lane – wide path, often grassy, between walls.

Information on sketch maps

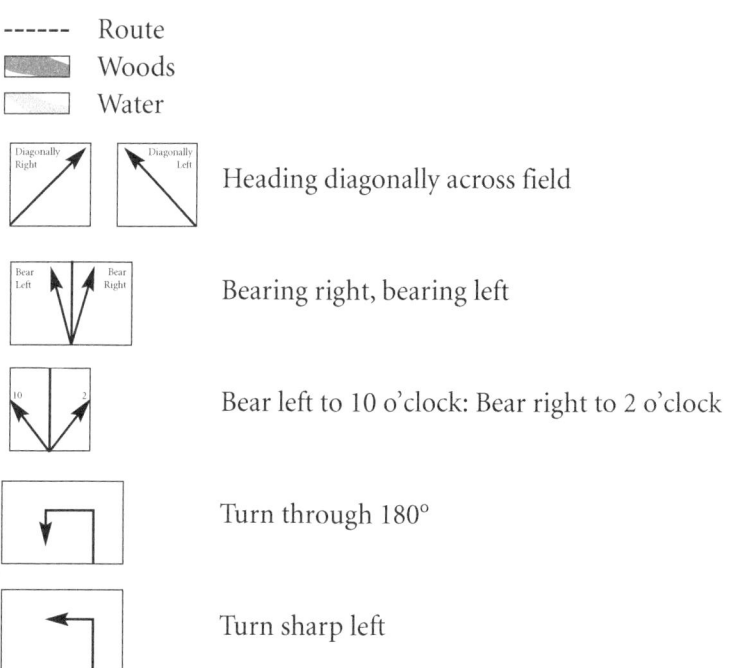

------ Route
Woods
Water

Heading diagonally across field

Bearing right, bearing left

Bear left to 10 o'clock: Bear right to 2 o'clock

Turn through 180°

Turn sharp left

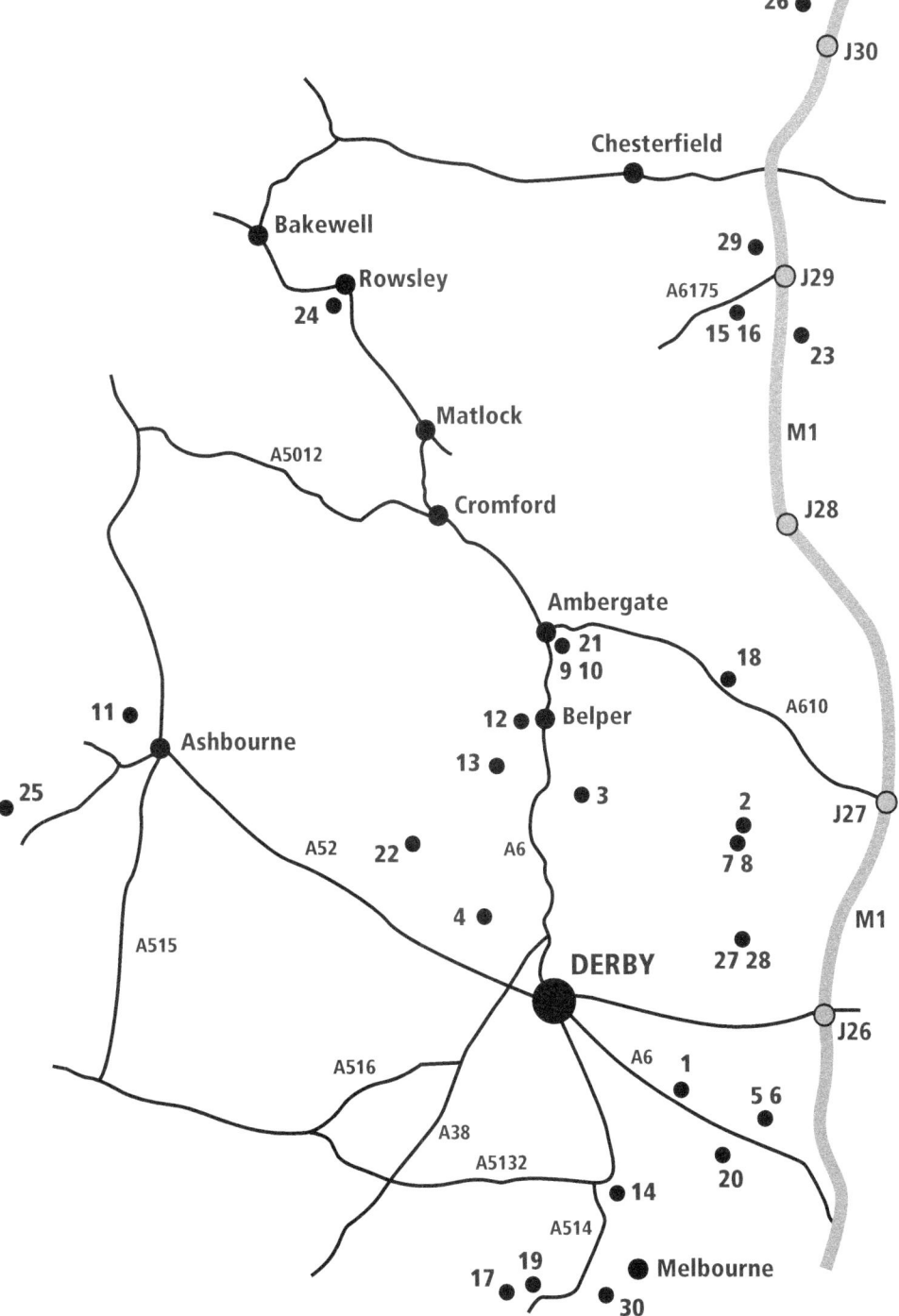

WALK 1
ELVASTON CASTLE

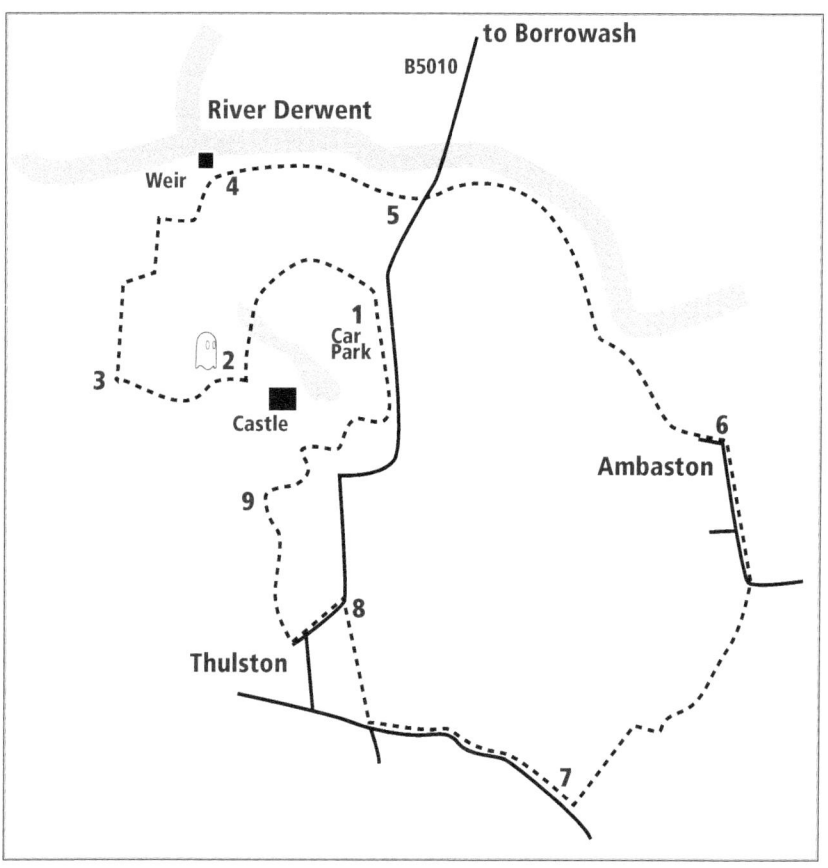

This is an easy flat walk, starting in the grounds of Elvaston Castle on good paths throughout. The scenery ranges from shady broadleaf woodland to lush fields and open views by the River Derwent.

Distance: 7¼ miles
Grade: A
Parking: From A52/Nottingham/Derby Road, take B5010 through Borrowash, following signs for Elvaston Castle. Turn right into car park. NB there is a small charge for parking.
Map Ref: SK 412332. Explorer 259 Derby Map.
Pub Stop: Teashop early in walk in Elvaston Castle. Pub stop at Thulston after 6 miles.

Route

1. From Elvaston Castle car park, return down access road towards the main road, but just before you reach it turn left on to a wide path. Go ahead on a pleasant woodland path. On reaching a lane, go straight over and continue ahead through the woodland. At the next track, again go ahead, following the sign for 'Park Centre & Castle'. Go across a stone bridge over an arm of the lake and down an avenue lined by rhododendrons. When you come to a track, turn left if you wish to visit the castle and tearooms, but you must return to this point to continue the walk.

While the exterior of Elvaston dates from Victorian times, it is only the latest in a series of buildings which go back to the 11th century.

The Institute of Paranormal research has carried out an investigation in the building, and their report makes fascinating reading on their website. Their researchers picked up a large amount of paranormal activity on the night that they spent there. Of particular note was the 'Gothic' Room, where a number of presences were felt to be moving around the room, and it was as though some sort of ceremony was taking place there. A picture from a camcorder left within the room was found to have been tilted through 15 degrees over a period of one and a half minutes. This could not be explained by the tripod tilting because the axis point is within the frame!

At a later séance in the same room another camcorder was again moved by unseen hands.

Elvaston Castle, the scene of a large amount of paranormal activity.

The 'Mirrored' Room had the presences of a 'terrified' maid and a 'strong' woman. While the researchers were in there, the door knob was rattled, although none of rest of their party were anywhere near at the time.

On a balcony running into the servants' quarters, one of the team felt as though he had been pushed sideways to the edge of the balcony. A little unnerving as there is drop of 25ft to a stone floor.

2. Otherwise turn right here to continue the walk. On reaching a corner where the Elvaston Castle Equestrian Centre is to the left, turn right off the paved road on to a track passing the equestrian centre training arenas on your left. Cross a bridge over a stream and ignore a footpath to the left.
3. At a crossroads on the path, pass through a kissing gate on the right and follow a tree-lined gravel path for about ½ mile to reach a weir on the River Derwent. This is a pleasant place to stop for a break.
4. Turn right on the broad track and continue for ½ mile. Where the track swings right away from the river, go ahead up a small slope, cross over the road and continue on the path by the river.
5. On reaching the next road (B5010), again go straight across and continue along the river (Derwent Valley Heritage Way) for about ¾ mile. Turn right at a sign where the footpath leaves the river, go down four steps through a hedge, then turn left and follow the arrow signs over three fields. At the end of the third field, go over a stile, not through an open gateway. Halfway down the fourth field, go over the stile to the left and follow the direction of the arrow across a field, towards the houses.
6. Go over a stile and down a broad green lane between houses. On reaching the road, turn right and walk down it. This is Main Street in the village of Ambaston. At the end of the houses keep straight ahead, ignoring the sign to the right for Elvaston. Where the road bends to the left, bear right at the sign for public bridleway, passing the water-filled old quarry workings on your right. Continue past the water, over a hump bridge and on to a green lane. After passing the quarry equipment, go through an iron gate following the hedge line on your left. The path swings right then back

left through another gate and then heads through Bellington Farm. Go straight through the farmyard, down a lane beyond to the road.

7. Turn right. Continue for just under ¾ mile. Just after the entrance to Thurlestone Grange on your right, turn right over a stile in the hedgerow and bear left across the field to a stile in the left corner. Go down the next field with the hedge on your left. On reaching the farm buildings (Grange Farm) continue ahead, ignoring the footpath sign to left. Where the track goes to the right continue ahead, following the footpath arrow on a wooden gate.

8. On reaching Oak Road, turn left. Continue past the Harrington Arms on your right (or stop for a pint!) and then on to Grove Close. Go over Brook Road then turn right just before the first house. Note there is no footpath sign at this point. With the fence on your left, go ahead emerging into a field. Continue ahead and go through a kissing gate (which does have a sign) then ahead to a second one into a broad field. At the end of this field, head for the imposing (original) gates to the castle.

9. On reaching the road, just before the gates, turn right. After 100 yards turn left, staying on this path as it bears right with woodland on your left. This track turns right and then left, emerging by a high brick wall. Where the path forks, keep right. A little further on there is the entrance to the Old English Garden on your right, which is well worth a visit. Continuing on past the garden, bear right on to a broad paved road. Just before you reach the main road ahead, turn left on to a signed bridleway into woodland. Continue on this track, which parallels the road until you reach the entrance to the car park where you turn left back to your car.

WALK 2
MAPPERLEY

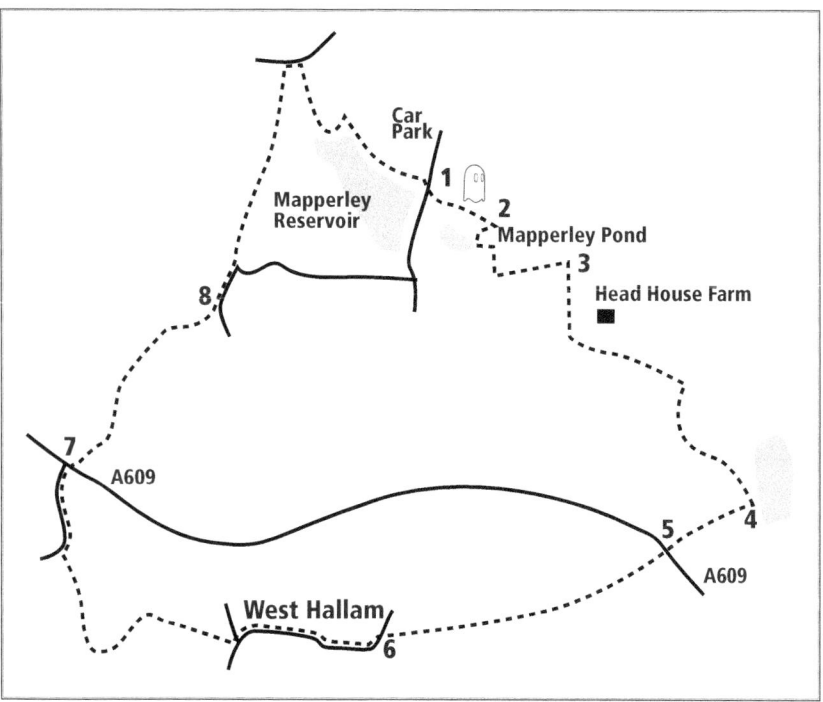

This is an easy walk to the west of Ilkeston, on good paths going through a variety of fields and woodland tracks. It is most attractive in springtime when the woods are filled with bluebells, although, if you wish to see our tragic ghost, he is said to appear on 25 October, the anniversary of his fiancée's death.

Both spring and autumn are good times for this walk. In midsummer views of Mapperley Pond are obscured by undergrowth and some of the lesser-used paths overgrown.

Distance: 7 miles
Grade: A
Parking: Car park adjacent to Shipley Country Park at Mapperley
            Reservoir. WCs in car park. Small parking charge – honesty
            box. Access is from A609 Ilkeston Road. Turn right at sign for
            Mapperley – Village and reservoir only.
Map Ref: SK 345437. Explorer 260 Nottingham Map.
Pub Stop: In West Hallam, approximately halfway around the walk, there
            are the Punchbowl and the White Hart pubs.

Route
1. From the car park, return to the access road, but leave it before it crosses
the end of the reservoir and choose a path to the left, labelled 'Nature
Reserve' (between road and a wide track to left). Go through this pleasant
woodland path, which is filled with bluebells in May time and birdsong.
When you reach a notice board for the nature reserve, turn right to visit
Mapperley Pond.

**Our ghost story concerns the tale of two young lovers and dates back to
the 1850s. Kate Usher was inconsolable when told that her fiancé, Giles
Kidbrooke, had been killed in action in the Crimea. In less than 12
months, she was found to have committed suicide by drowning herself
in Mapperley Pond. It is even more tragic, therefore, that the report of
Giles's death was incorrect. He had been badly wounded and it was a
considerable time before he was well enough to return home. On hearing
of Kate's suicide he was devastated. He died a few years later, having
never married and become a recluse.**

**His ghost has been seen on the anniversary of Kate's death (25
October) as he circles the lake in a ghostly coach, peering forlornly from
it, looking for his love. Villagers in Mapperley saw him frequently in the
1940s and 1950s as he travelled between the Black Horse Pub, the lake
and a second inn, known as the Candlestick, which you will reach later
in the walk.**

Mapperley Pond, the site of a tragic love story.

2. Return to the path, turn right and continue in the same direction as before. Continue ahead until you exit the reserve, going on to a (muddy) track, where you turn right. Go over a wooden bridge, round a right hand bend, over a second bridge and then re-enter the nature reserve through a low iron gate on your right. Follow this woodland path, and where it bends to the left look to your right for another view of Mapperley Pond. Stay on this path until you reach another low iron gate where you exit on to a track and turn right. When you reach a T junction, turn left following the sign for 'Shipley Wood'. The structures protruding into the skyline to your left are in the American Adventure theme park.

3. When you reach a track on your right, turn on to it and continue, passing Head House Farm on your left. As the track starts to go down the hill, go over a stile on your left and cross the field, following the direction of the arrow to a stile in the far corner. Cross the farm track and over the stile on the far side. Go down this field with the hedge on your right, over two stiles and go straight ahead across the next field to a gap to be seen on the far side. Go on to the bridge and turn right over a stile on to a path into the trees. Keep straight ahead through this woodland, paralleling the stream on your right. NB if doing the walk in summer, this path may be overgrown with nettles and brambles. In this case, an alternative is to turn left through a gap in the hedge about 30 yards after crossing the stile. Turn right along the hard track and continue to the bridge. The path eventually emerges on to a lane where you go under the bridge and follow the paved path as it winds right and left, reaching a lake on your left. This is a pleasant place for a break.

4. About three-quarters of the way along the lake, turn right over a wooden bridge, at a sign saying 'Danger electricity cables' and an arrow for the 'Centenary Way'. Go into Pewit Carr Nature Reserve on a tarmac path. Where the path bends sharply left, leave the path and go ahead over a stile into a field, where houses may be seen in the distance. Proceed up the field with the fence on your right until you reach a barn, where you turn left and then right along the side of it, finally reaching the road.

5. Turn left, then after 50 yards turn right by the side of no.136, still following signs for the 'Centenary Way'. Cross the first field with the hedge on your left. In the next field, after 30 yards turn left and go over a stile in the hedge. Turn right and continue forward, now with the hedge on your right for the remainder of this field and the following three, at the end of which you enter a green lane. The lane eventually leads you to the road in West Hallam.

6. Turn left and proceed through the village, passing the entrance to St Wilfrid's Church and the Punchbowl pub (or go in – it's open seven days a week). At the far end of the village, ignore two footpaths to the right, then when you see the White Hart pub ahead cross over the road and go past it (or again call in), and then turn immediately right on to a green lane, following an arrow for the 'Centenary Way'. At the end of the green lane, go ahead into the field, walking with the hedge on your right. Three quarters of the way along this field, when you reach a stile on your right, do NOT go over the stile. Instead bear left across the field, heading to the left of the electricity pylon to a stile in the corner. Following a sign for the 'Centenary Way', go down the field with the fence on your left. Go over the stile at the end and take a path bearing right up to the copse. On reaching a wide track at the top of the hill, turn sharp right and go down this track (NB a cart track which hugs the hedge on your right from the last stile leads to the same place but is not the designated right of way.) Stay on this broad track until it reaches a road. Turn right and continue until you reach the main A609 road.

7. Cross over the road and turn right then almost immediately left at a public footpath sign. Go between the buildings into a green lane and then turn right at the footpath sign on to a narrow path, passing the end of the cottage, winding between hedges over a stile into a field. Turn left and go up this field and the next one, with the hedge on your left. In the third field, bear right, passing a stile to your left by a wooden gate and heading for a stile to the left of the water trough. Go up the next two fields. In the following field, bear right, keeping the windsock on your right, to a white sign to be seen in the hedge saying 'Beware Aircraft'. Go over the stile and bear slightly right in the next field, crossing the mown airstrip to a stile in the hedge opposite. Cross a second stile then continue straight down the field to the stile to the right of the bottom left corner. When you reach the road, turn left. Where the road bends right, leave it and go straight ahead on a paved track.

The third of the properties on the road to the right was originally the second pub mentioned in our tragic love story. Originally called the Royal Oak, it was better known as Candlesticks, a name it still bears today as a private house.

8. Go over the stile at the end of the lane into the field, then follow the yellow arrow marker and, taking a line parallel to the hedge on your right, proceed down this large field to the stile in the centre of the bottom hedge. Continue in the same direction down the next field, then in the following one bear slightly right, heading to the right of a red-brick house to be seen in the trees. Go over a stile in the hedge into a potholed lane and turn right then almost immediately right again, following signs for 'Circular Walk 18' and 'Amber Valley 16'. Go ahead on a broad path through lovely woodland, with drifts of bluebells in the spring and an accompaniment of birdsong. When you reach a T junction turn left over a wooden bridge, then keep left at the next junction. The path winds at the side of Mapperley Reservoir. Continue along it until you reach some low wooden steps on your left. Go up these and back into the car park.

WALK 3
HOLBROOK

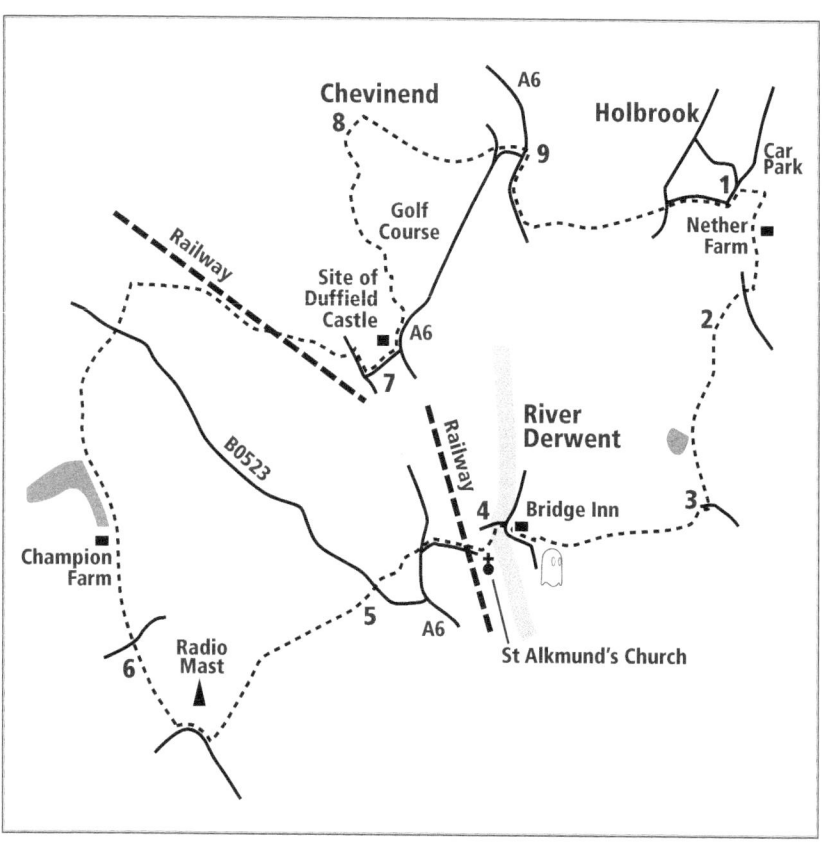

Good views of rolling countryside and a variety of fields, woods and rivers make up this more demanding walk that circles the town of Duffield, which lies to the south of Belper. The strange story of the Devil dictating the site of the church adds the ghostly interest.

Distance: 10 miles
Grade: C
Parking: In Holbrook, at the bottom of Moorside Lane or on a stretch of road between the junction at the bottom of Moorside Lane and the telephone box.
Map Ref: Start SK 364449. Parking SK 365450 to SK 365448. Explorer 259 Derby map.
Pub Stop: The Bridge Inn on the River Derwent is reached after two miles and in the latter part of the walk at Milford there is the Strutt Arms, the Kingwell Inn and the Hollybush Inn at the top of Hollybush Lane. There is also the Spotted Cow adjacent to the parking in Holbrook.

Route
1. Just north of the Spotted Cow pub, on the opposite side of the road, is Stoney Lane, opposite house no.8 and the Gaslight Gallery.

Note the fascinating ceramic over the doorway of this wonderfully old-fashioned shop, which was once owned by Charles Forster and is now run by his wife. A talented potter, he specialised in houses, trains, trams, toilets and tarts, all of which are depicted in the ceramic over the door if you look carefully.

Go down Stoney Lane past Hillside Cottage. When you reach a track to the right, turn on to it and go ahead on a broad track. Go past Nether Farm and continue on this lane until you reach the road. Turn right, then after 50 yards turn left through a gap stile in the wall with a footpath sign for the 'Derwent Valley Way'. Follow the direction of the footpath sign across the field to the top left corner on to a path into the edge of the woodland and a gap stile. Cross an ancient-looking bridge, up stone steps, into the field and left through a gap stile into the lane. Turn right.
2. After passing Day Park Cottage on your right, go over a stile into the field, then diagonally right across the field to the stone wall in the corner.

St Alkmund's Church. The Devil dictated where it should be built.

Go over a stile then over a second stile by an iron gate and bear left across the field to the copse. Go over a stone stile, keep to the right for 50 yards and then go over a wooden stile into the next field where you walk adjacent to the hedge on your left. Go through the stile and straight across to where the field dips down to a stile into the wood. After 20 yards you reach a path crossing your own, with a stile to the left. Do NOT go over the stile. Instead, turn right up the slope, following broken signs above on a tree for the 'Centenary Way'.

3. This woodland path emerges into fields where you walk with the hedge on your left, passing through two gates. When you go through a third gate, cross the stile on your left, turn right and continue forward, now with the hedge on your right. Go over a stile at the end on to a woodland path. Leave the wood at the sign for the 'Centenary Way', bearing left where paths cross. Descend steeply down the path and steps, keeping straight ahead at the public bridleway sign to emerge by some cottages, and continue ahead to a road. Turn right down the hill to the Bridge Inn. Turn left over the bridge, following the sign for Duffield and Derby. On the far side of the bridge, turn left at the public footpath sign, just before Derwent Bridge Cottage. Go along a path by the river for a short distance, over a stile, then cross the field heading for the cross of the war memorial. Turn left to visit St Alkmund's Church. There is a bench just inside the churchyard, which makes a pleasant place for a break.

This place was not the original choice for the church in Duffield. It was to be built on a small hill adjacent to the ruins of Duffield Castle, which you will visit later in the walk. Building materials were taken to this site and work commenced. However, the Devil had other plans and workers arrived one day to find that everything had been removed to the other side of the village by the river. The wood and stone were brought back and foundations laid, but again by the next day all had been transported back to the river.

Convinced that evil forces were at work, prayers were said at the original site and work recommenced but to no avail. Each day materials

were laboriously brought back and the work redone and by night all was undone and transported back to the site by the river.

This battle continued for some time, but in the end it was the Devil who won the day as the church authorities finally gave in and built the church on its present site. Why the Devil should have objected to the other site is not known, but cottages built later on that site were said to be haunted most nights by a 'bogey', so perhaps it was a meeting place for evil spirits that the Devil did not want disrupted.

4. From the war memorial, take the bridge over the railway. On the far side, go to the right, ignoring the public footpath sign to the left and ignoring a sign to the right after a few yards for the 'Midshires Way'. Keep ahead down the lane to a road where you turn left. At the corner, bear left following the sign for 'Allestree'. On reaching the main A6 road, cross straight over on to a public footpath between the walls. Where it emerges into a close, bear left and continue between houses at a sign saying 'No cycling, No Horses.'

Duffield Castle, where the Devil opposed building a church.

At a T junction, turn right. When you reach the road, turn right again then almost immediately left at a public footpath sign between nos.17 and 19. Go between the fences to emerge on a main road (B5023). Turn left and almost immediately right at a public footpath sign. Go over a stile into a field and straight ahead. Go over a stile in the corner and turn right (do not turn right on the path before the stile).

5. Go straight ahead with the hedge on your right and continue across two more fields. Go through the gate and three further fields with the hedge on your right. Go over the stile in the top right-hand corner with the radio mast to your right. Bear slightly left, but not on the cart track, to pick up the yellow arrow marker situated on the left edge of the trees. On reaching a lane, turn right. On reaching a main road (The Common), again turn right. Just after a left-hand bend in the road and a white cottage, turn right at a public footpath sign. Keep to the right-hand side of the field. Go over a double stile into the next field where you walk with the hedge on your right. At the end of the field, turn on to the footpath to the right (not straight ahead), then continue forward with the hedge on your left for the next two fields until you reach a road.

6. Turn right and almost immediately left at a public footpath sign and also a sign for 'Champion Farm'. Go ahead on a broad cart track to 'Champion Farm'. Go past the farm followed by a woodland dell to your left, which is carpeted with bluebells in May time. Keep ahead on the cart track until you eventually reach a road (B5023). Turn right and immediately left at the public footpath sign and follow the direction of the sign across a field. Cross over the stile and head straight across the next field. On the far side, go through a stile and across the wooden bridge over the stream, then turn immediately right. Cross the field heading to 11 o'clock, in a line roughly towards the red-brick houses on the horizon, to a stile by a loop of the stream to your right. Cross the stile and go straight ahead over the field. In the following two fields, walk adjacent to the hedge on your left. In the next, the fourth, after 100 yards turn left over a stile and take care as you cross the railway. Go over the stile on the far side and turn right, following the direction of the arrow. Go straight across the second field and bear left on entering the third, passing a cemetery to your left. Go over a stile and along a path between bushes to reach ornate gates on your right, then keep left up a tarmac lane between a hedge and a brick wall to reach the road.

7. Turn right. Go past Lime Avenue on your left and continue dropping down the hill until you reach Castle Hill where you turn left. Go up Castle Hill and down the other side. When you reach the main A6 road, turn left. After about 15 yards watch for a sign on the left for 'Duffield Castle'.

Duffield Castle. On this site stood a Norman castle built by the Ferrers family. The keep, 95ft by 93ft with walls up to 15ft thick, was as large as any in England. Occupied in turn by Celts, Romans and Saxons, the fortress once covered five acres.

Go up the steps to the left of the notice to view the remaining stones of this site, which makes a pleasant place for an afternoon break.

Note that it was adjacent to this site that the church authorities wished to build the original Duffield Church. In the afternoon sunshine it seems an innocuous place for a battle between good and evil.

After returning to the road, turn left. Cross Avenue Road and go on to a path between Avenue Road and the A6, marked 'Midshires Way'. Go down the access road to the golf course and turn right at a public footpath sign at the end of the clubhouse. Go up a broad tarmac lane with the golf course on your right. Where a stone wall on your right ends, leave the track and turn left at a public footpath sign marked 'Midshires Way'. Cross two fields with a hedge on your right. Pass through an open gateway and across a bridge over a stream and bear left in a third field with a copse on your right. Go through a gate stile at the end of the field and continue up a green lane. Bear left upwards through the field.

At the top, go over the stile in the wall and keep ahead up the hill, ignoring paths to the right and left. Cross a track and continue steeply uphill following the Midshires Way. Cross an access path to the golf course and ascend the very last bit of the hill to reach a deeply-rutted track at Chevinend. Stop to catch your breath and admire the view.

8. Turn right and stay on this lane, ignoring tracks to the left and the right, until you reach the houses. Keep straight ahead then steeply downhill. When you reach the bottom of Sunny Hill, opposite the Belper Milford Primary School, turn right down to the main A6 road opposite the Strutt Arms in Milford. Turn left. Cross the River Derwent, then where the A6 turns sharp left at the King William pub, turn right following the sign for Makeney.

Note the Ebenezer Chapel dated 1859 on your left adjacent to the pub. Now a holiday cottage, it sleeps 22 and costs in excess of £1,300 pw.

9. Stay on this road past the Riverside Garden Centre. Then, just past the Makeney Hall Hotel and Restaurant, turn left up Hollybush Lane. After a short rise, turn right and immediately left on the public footpath between walls (before you come to the Hollybush Inn). Climb the steps and go straight up the field to a 'V'-shaped wooden gap stile. In the second field, walk with the hedge to your right. Go over the stile into a third field and walk straight across, then, in the two following fields, continue with the hedge on your right, leading eventually on to a road. Turn left and then immediately right at a sign for Coxbench and Holbrook on Mellors Lane. Go down the lane. When you reach the road at the telephone box, turn left back to where you are parked.

WALK 4
KEDLESTON PARK

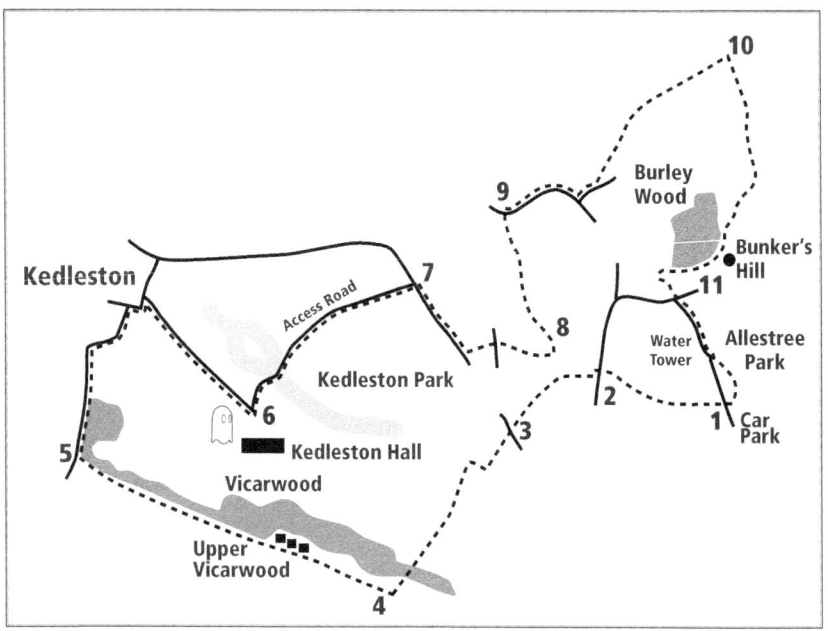

This is a most enjoyable undulating walk with panoramic views in an area to the north east of Derby. It takes in Kedleston Park with a chance to visit the hall and gardens.

Distance: 9 miles

Grade: B

Parking: Car park on the edge of Allestree Park on Woodlands Lane. Access is easiest to find from the main road in Quarndon. Woodlands Lane lies to the east of the church.

Map Ref: SK 341404. Explorer 259 Derby Map.

Pub Stop: None.

Kedleston Hall, which houses only benign ghosts.

Access to Kedleston Park is free if you are just walking through. There is a charge for visiting the hall and gardens. National Trust members get in free. The park is open all year round. Hall and gardens open March to October. Check the website for times and charges.

Route

1. Leave the car park and turn right on the road, then turn left at a public footpath after 30 yards. Go straight ahead along the track and down the field. Continue in the same direction in the next field with the hedge on your right. At the far end, go through a gap to your right then turn left to continue in the same direction as before, now with the hedge on your left. Go over a stile and continue ahead with the wall on your left, then go over another stile on to a road. Cross over and turn left, then after 20 yards turn right at the public footpath sign.

2. Go between the wall and the hedge and then ahead over the stile into a field. Bear left towards the gap in the fence at the top of the field. When you reach the gateway, go into the field adjacent to the hedge on the left. Where the hedge goes left, continue by the side of it. At the end of the field, go over the stile in the corner. Go over the footbridge and ahead in the next field, again with the hedge on your left to reach a stile on to a road.

3. Cross over and into the field, now with hedge on your right. At the bottom of the field go right, over a stile (or through the gap if it is overgrown). With the hedge on your right, go along the top of the field then left at the end to continue down the field, then cross the footbridge with an arrow marker. Go straight up the next (large) field, through a gap in the hedge and continue straight ahead up the following field (there are no markers and it may have been ploughed). Go through a gap in the hedge into the woodland and continue straight ahead in the following field until you reach a paved track.

4. Turn right. Stay on this track for ½ mile. Pass the buildings of Upper Vicarwood on your right, and then go through an iron gate and ahead on a wide track at a public footpath sign. Continue on this broad track for another ¾ mile until you reach an iron gate leading on to a road.

5. Turn right. Stay on the road, passing the sign for 'Kedleston' until you reach a T junction. Turn right, following the sign for 'Kedleston Hall'. Go round a left-hand bend and then after 50 yards turn right at the sign for Kedleston Hall. Go straight up the access road and ignore the road to the left. You eventually reach a T junction with 'Kedleston Hall' to your right.

Kedleston Hall was designed by Robert Adam in the late 18th century for the Curzon family and is a fine example of the neoclassical style much favoured at that time.

Kedleston is not overrun with spirits, and those it has are said to be benign. There have, however, been occasions when footsteps have been heard in the upper rooms or doors closed unaccountably. There have been feelings of being watched or being spoken to by an unseen presence and the sound of heavy breathing heard in the saloon.

The family occupy the east wing, and it is said to be haunted by a poltergeist that throws things about or moves their possessions.

It is thought that all these happenings can be attributed to Mrs Garnett, who was housekeeper from 1766 to 1809 and who took great pride in showing visitors around the hall.

A female worker, on two separate occasions, saw a pale ghostly figure walking unhappily in the gardens. This was believed to be the ghost of Thomas Chatterton, an English poet, whose statue lies in a passageway of the hall, although it is not known what his connection is to Kedleston.

6. Turn left. Go over a bridge (a pleasant place to stop for a break by the river) and ahead up the road or walk adjacent to it on the grass. Where the road forks, keep right to eventually leave the park.

7. Turn right and take care on this busy road. Pass the entrance to the golf club and a sign for a hotel then turn left at a public footpath sign, over a stile into a field. Bear right across a field (not following the direction of the sign) heading for a big tree, then bear left to a stile hidden in the hedge. Go over the stile, cross the lane and over another stile into a field. Follow the direction of the arrow up the field and over a stile at the corner of the fence. Follow the arrow sign to walk with hedge on your left. Drop down a hill, over a stile, then cross the footbridge and go over a second stile. Continue ahead in the field with the hedge on your right.

8. Just before the next stile, turn sharp left heading back diagonally across the field. When you reach the boundary, go through a gap in the hedge and then to the right. Go over a stile in the corner and continue ahead in the field, walking parallel to the fence on the right. At the far side, go left, following the arrow sign, then turn right through a gap stile. Go straight across the field. Pass where the hedge comes in from the right, to a gap stile in the corner. Continue ahead in the next field with the hedge on your right. At the far end go over two stiles to reach a road.

9. Turn right. Ignore the first footpath to the left by a white cottage. Go round a right-hand bend, then turn left at a lane with a public footpath sign. Pass the house on the left, then leave the lane to go left over a stile. Go ahead in the field, then past the trees on your left. Near the end of the trees, at a yellow arrow sign, bear right to the hedge ahead of you (ignoring the track). The stile is hidden in the fence behind it. Go over the stile and keep straight ahead for five fields. Cross the sixth field.

10. On the far side, ignore the stile to the left. Instead, turn right along the bottom hedge to walk with it on your left. At the end, go over a footbridge, then turn right on the lane and immediately left at the public footpath sign. Go up the field with the hedge on your right. Pass the footpath signs and then, at end of field, turn right through a gap and cross the next field. Go over the stile and turn right, up the centre of the following field with a house to your right. Continue uphill with the trees of Burley Wood to your right. The path continues by the side of the trees. It is, however, worth diverting slightly to the left to climb to the highest point, which is Bunker's Hill. Here you will find a topograph showing you what lies in all directions at this panoramic viewpoint. From the viewpoint, rejoin the path at the side of the wood to reach a stile at the right-hand end of the houses. Go along the path between the fence and the wood then ahead on a green lane. When you reach a path on the left, turn left down it to reach a road. Turn left and continue to the main road.

11. Turn right and immediately left down Woodlands Lane. Pass the water tower, then 100 yards further on turn left at a public footpath sign into the wood. After 10 yards, take the first footpath to the right. Cross the open area with the picnic tables and go back into the trees at the bottom-left corner. Bear right through the trees and, where the path divides, take the right-hand fork and continue ahead to reach the car park.

WALK 5 AND 6
CHURCH WILNE

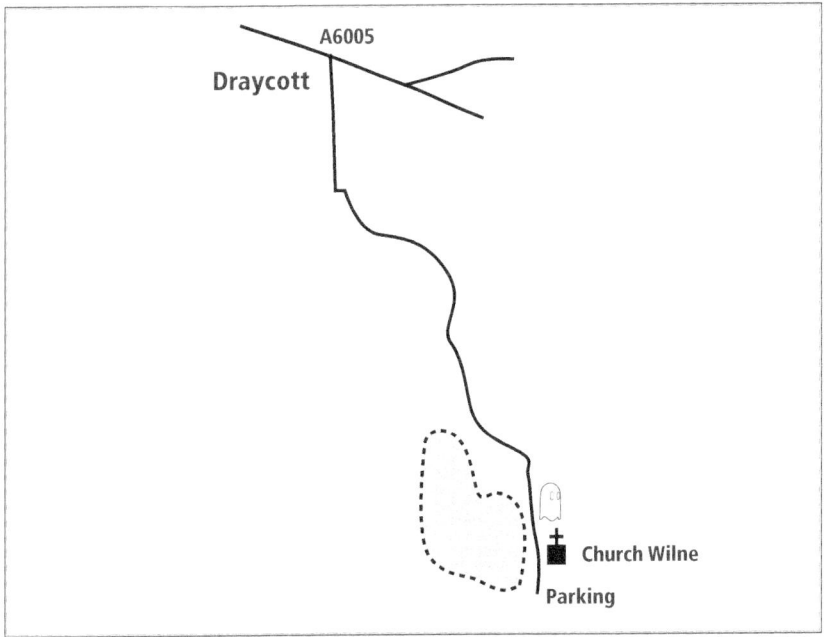

A short but pleasant walk around St Chads Water at Church Wilne, with a chance to hear some ghostly organ music.

Distance: 1 mile

Grade: A

Parking: From the A6005 in Draycott, go down Market Street. Keep straight on where it says single track road. Continue ahead for about a mile until you reach the church. Opposite this there is a parking area called St Chads Water car park.

Map Ref: SK 448318. Explorer 260 Nottingham Map.

Pub Stop: None.

Church Wilne is haunted by a tragic organist.

Route

1. With your back to the entrance of the car park, leave it bearing right to the top right-hand corner towards the water. Turn right on to a paved path. Where the path forks, keep left to remain by the water, rejoining the right-hand path a little further on. Stay on this track as it circles the lake, going from paved to boarding to a woodland path. When you finally reach a bench in memory of Wilf Murray, turn right back to the car park.

Take time to visit the church across the road. It is very pretty inside and is used occasionally for weddings and funerals. It is open each Sunday for Evensong from Easter until October when it closes except for Christmas Midnight Mass.

It is said that at times 'haunting' but sad organ music emanates from inside its locked interior. The church and Wilne Lane are said to be haunted by the ghost of Martin Astle, who killed himself after a failed love affair. Late one night, he went to the church and sat playing the organ for a while before proceeding to the old mill and hanging himself from a beam. It was on the road to the right (when facing the church) that a courting couple were parked one evening in September 1988. Their cuddling was rudely interrupted when they saw a young man dressed in Victorian clothes walk towards them. He appeared to have come from the church. His attire would have been surprise enough, but he then passed through the wing of the car and continued down the road towards the old mill, which is further down the same road.

A lady in grey also haunts a house in Wilne Lane. This is said to be a Victorian girl, Jeanette Soresby, who died when only 20. The restaurant, the Lady in Grey, in Shardlow is named after this ghost.

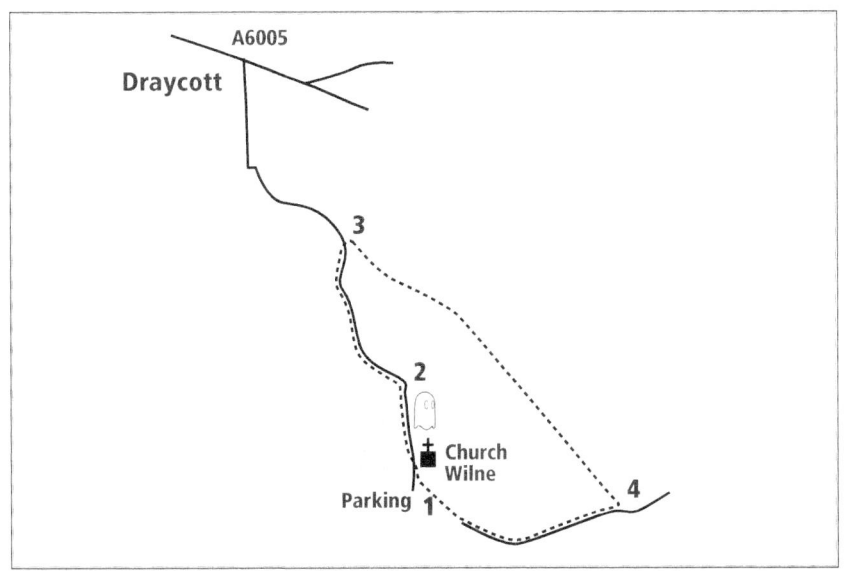

This second route is an easy two-mile walk on good paths. A tragic young man and a haunted church add the ghostly interest. (See Walk 5)

Distance: 2 miles

Grade: A

Parking: From the A6005 in Draycott, go down Market Street. Keep straight on where it says single track road. Continue ahead for about a mile until you reach the church. Opposite this, there is a parking area called St Chads Water car park.

Map Ref: SK 448318. Explorer 260 Nottingham Map.

Pub Stop: None.

Route

1. With your back to the entrance to the car park, leave it bearing right to the top right-hand corner towards the water. Turn right on to a paved path. Where the path forks, keep left to remain by the water, rejoining the right-hand path a little further on. Pass the carved duck and the seat for Roy Cudworth and Mistie, then as you reach the end of the water on your left, turn right under a wire in a gap in the hedge and under the power lines.

2. Continue straight ahead to walk with a hedge on your right-hand side. At the end of the hedge go up a small bank, then down the other side, bearing right on to a path. After 15 yards, turn left where the path forks. The path joins the River Derwent. Where the river starts to curve to the left and the wooden fencing on your right ends, turn right towards an iron gate. Go up a short rise, cross the road and through the stile on the far side.

3. Go ahead on the broad top of the flood bank. Go over two stiles. After the second one, cross a path and over a stile opposite, on the Midshires Way. Continue ahead on the grassy path. At the point where this swings left, bear right down the slope to a stile to be seen below. (NB there are no markers at this point.) Go ahead with a hedge on your right until you reach a stile leading you on to Wilne Lane.

4. Turn right. Pass under power lines and round a bend. Pass a lay-by on your left, then where the road bends left go on to a footpath on your right, following the direction of the arrow across the field. Note the old mill over to your left. This is the mill mentioned in the ghost story, see Walk 5. Go over the stile on the far side with a wire fence on your right to reach the road, where you turn right past the church back to the car park.

WALK 7 AND 8 SHIPLEY PARK

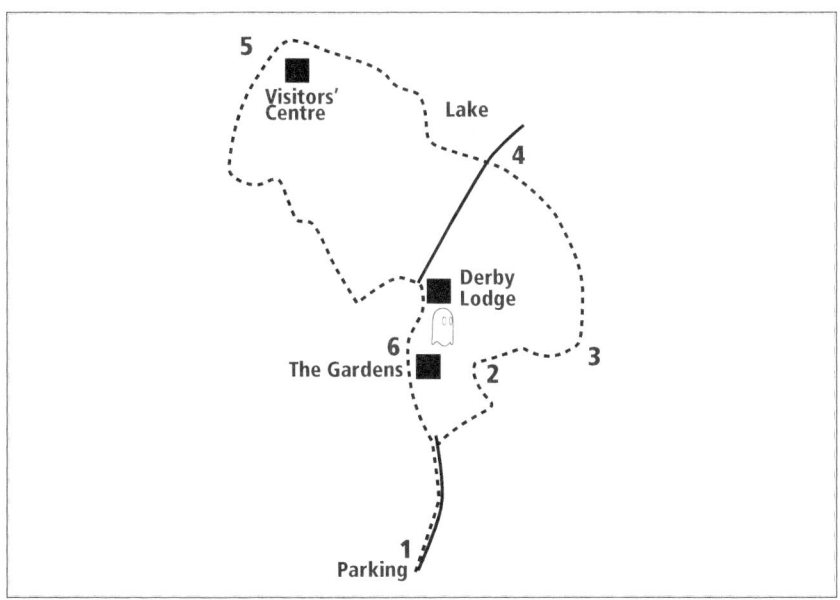

This is the shorter version of Walk 8 and is a pleasant easy walk, mostly on good tracks and paths with only a few fields to cross. It has a choice of two refreshment stops, a variety of terrain and a host of ghost stories to spice it up (also see Walk 8).

Distance: 3¼ miles

Grade: A

Parking: Car park adjacent to Shipley Country Park at Mapperley Reservoir. WCs in car park. Small parking charge – honesty box. Access is from A609 Ilkeston Road. Turn right at the sign for Mapperley – village and reservoir only.

Map Ref: SK 345437. Explorer 260 Nottingham Map.

Pub Stop: No pub, but refreshments are available at the visitors' centre and also at Derby Lodge on Sundays. Open 11am–4.30pm throughout the year.

Route

1. Return to the entrance of the car park and turn left up the road. Walk on the grassy bridleway at the side if you prefer. When you reach the wood on your right, turn into it, bearing left uphill (i.e. not on the path to the right). At the top of the rise, when you reach a path crossing your own, turn left. Go ahead through the magnificent mature trees to reach the water tower.

This stone tower was built in 1884 to supply water to the hall and gardens, Home Farm and the nearby village of Shipley. It is now a private residence. The large iron tank remains in the structure and is now a bedroom. The smaller brick tower is a more recent addition and acts as a staircase for the house.

The path curves round to the right. Go ahead to the information board, which gives details and a plan of Shipley Hall as it was. See Walk 8 for ghostly tales.

2. Facing the information board, go on to the path on your left and pass down the side of the ruins of the foundations of the hall and along the bottom. The path curves left and is attractive in May time when it is lined with rhododendrons. When you reach a T junction, turn right. At the next T junction, turn left to walk with the fence on your right (i.e. staying within the woodland).

Go out through a stile to your right, then turn immediately 180° left i.e. through the gap by the gateway to the right of the 'Shipley Park Visitor Centre' sign. Go past Nottingham Lodge, one of two identical lodges on the estate.

3. When you come to a broad track, cross it, bearing slightly right past the bench which says 'You'll never walk alone', to a Z-shaped gap in the fencing. Go straight ahead down the field. Cross the next field in the same direction. Go through the open gateway at the end, crossing a path, and continue ahead in field three. The path veers left in field four.

4. When you reach a road, turn right then left at the sign for the visitors' centre through the kissing gate. Walk with the lake to your right along a broad track. Continue to follow the sign for the visitors' centre where the path divides, staying by the lake. At the end of the lake, when the path forks again, keep left. Walk straight ahead where a path crosses your own. Go ahead into the car park of the visitors' centre then past the tourist information board, following the signs to the centre, café, toilets and gift shop. The Ramblers café serves a variety of drinks, snacks, light meals and cakes.

5. Leave the centre by the patio area behind the café, with the children's swings on your left. Walk along a wide path in front of you. Go past an adventure playground on your left. The path winds left, right and left again, and continues beside a young woodland on your left. When the path forks, keep right. When you reach a T junction, turn left and continue until you reach a lane and Derby Lodge, where you turn right.

Derby Lodge serves cream teas, homemade cakes, hot and cold drinks and ice creams. It is open on Sundays only, 11am–4.30pm. Its entrance is a few yards up the lane and through the gateway to your left.

A former tenant of Derby Lodge heard a child's footsteps upstairs one evening. She went to investigate thinking her daughter had got out of bed. However, the child was fast asleep and there was no sign of the ghostly visitor.

6. Go up the lane. When you reach a wooden gate on your right, opposite the buildings of Home Farm, leave the road and bear right on to a narrow woodland path. After 100 yards look to your left to see the mock Tudor building called The Gardens. (See Walk 8 for more ghostly tales.)

Where the path rejoins the road, keep to the right and continue down the hill back to the car park.

The Gardens, Shipley Park, is haunted by three ghosts.

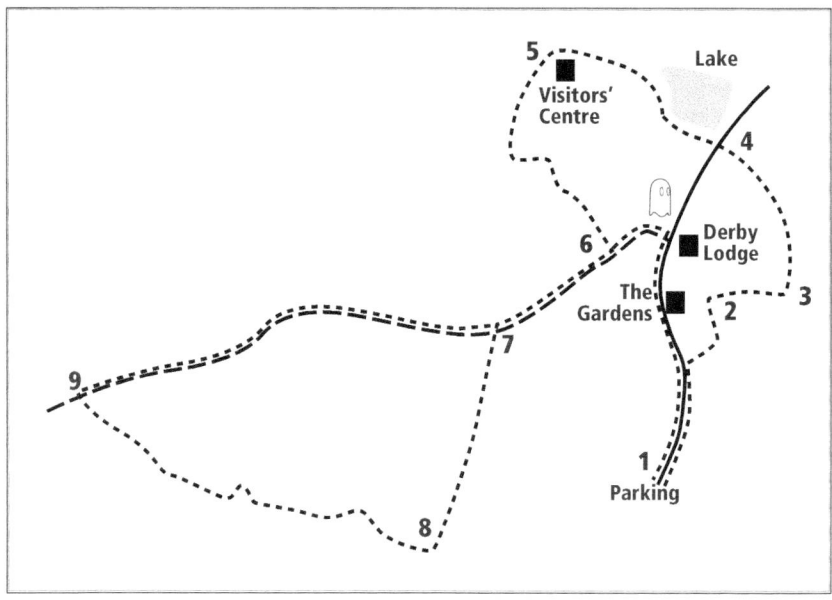

This is a longer version of Walk 7 and is a pleasant, easy walk, mostly on good tracks and paths with only a few fields to cross. It has open views and the chance of an encounter with a strange mist within the environs of Shipley Park, as well as a host of other ghostly tales.

Distance: 6¾ miles

Grade: A

Parking: Car park adjacent to Shipley Country Park at Mapperley Reservoir. WCs in car park. Small parking charge – honesty box. Access is from A609 Ilkeston Road. Turn right at sign for Mapperley – village and reservoir only.

Map Ref: SK 345437. Explorer 260 Nottingham Map.

Pub Stop: No pub but refreshments available at the visitors' centre. Also at Derby Lodge, on Sundays only. Open 11am–4.30pm throughout the year.

Route

1. Return to the entrance of the car park and turn left up the road. Walk on the grassy bridleway at the side if you prefer. When you reach the wood on your right, turn into it, bearing left uphill (i.e. not on the path to the right). At the top of the rise, when you reach a path crossing your own, turn left. Go ahead through the magnificent mature trees to reach the water tower.

The path curves round to the right. Go ahead to the information board which gives details and a plan of Shipley Hall as it was.

There are numerous ghostly tales associated with Shipley Park. In the 1970s a company of Girl Guides camping in the area where you are standing reported ghostly visitations.

Early one morning, in September 1991, when John Pratt entered the gates of Shipley Park to deliver milk, he noticed a strange mist hovering over the gates. John's border collie was beside him in the van, and when he drove beneath the mist it threw the dog Brumas back into the seat with great force. John experienced an intense cold. Normally the dog would run beside the van, but on this occasion it refused to move.

John experienced the vapour a second time when out with his wife and two friends. This time it was a pleasant summer evening and the mist kept pace with them, travelling along in the hedge.

2. Facing the information board, go on to the path on your left and pass down the side of the ruins of the foundations of the hall and along the bottom. The path curves left and is attractive in May time when it is lined with rhododendrons. When you reach a T junction, turn right. At the next T junction, turn left to walk with the fence on your right (i.e. staying within the woodland).

Go out through a stile to your right, then turn immediately 180° left (i.e. through the gap by the gateway to the right of the 'Shipley Park Visitor Centre' sign). Go past Nottingham Lodge, one of two identical Lodges on the estate.

3. When you come to a broad track, cross it, bearing slightly right past the bench which says 'You'll never walk alone', to a Z-shaped gap in the fencing. Go straight ahead down the field. Cross the next field in the same direction. Go through the open gateway at the end, crossing a path, and continue ahead in field three. The path veers left in field four.

4. When you reach a road, turn right and then left at the sign for the visitors' centre through the kissing gate. Walk with the lake to your right along a broad track. Continue to follow the sign for the visitors' centre where the path divides, staying by the lake. At the end of the lake, when the path forks again, keep left. Walk straight ahead where a path crosses your own. Go ahead into the car park of the visitors' centre then past the tourist information board, following the signs to the centre, café, toilets and gift shop. The Ramblers café serves a variety of drinks, snacks, light meals and cakes.

5. Leave the centre by the patio area behind the café, with the children's swings on your left. Walk along a wide path in front of you. Go past an adventure playground on your left. The path winds left, right and left again and continues beside a young woodland on your left. When the path forks, keep right. When you reach a T junction, turn right following the sign for 'Mapperley Reservoir'.

6. Pass a track on your right, then after 200 yards ignore an unmarked path to your left (with a wood on the right of it). Pass another path to the left between wooden fencing that has an arrow sign for 'Route 18' on it, pointing straight ahead up the lane you are on. Then after 30 yards, turn left at a stile in the hedge marked 'Route 18'.

7. Go over the field on an indistinct path. There are two lone trees on the far side, which you should keep to your left. The path then dips down to a stile in the hedge. Cross a small stream and over another stile. Follow the direction of the arrow in the next field, then in the following large field proceed up the centre of it.

8. When you reach an arrow sign in an open gateway, turn right over a stile in the hedge. Walk diagonally across the field, bearing left away from the hedge on your right, to a stile in the left-hand fencing, 50 yards from the top-left corner. Go through the woodland and over a stile on to the lane beyond.

Turn right. Go over a stile by a gate at the end of the lane and straight ahead with a hedge on your left. Cross over a stile at the far end and round to the right with a small copse on your right. Pass under some power lines, over a stile, then turn right through the hedge on your right BEFORE the open gateway. Go over a stile and through the next field, with the hedge on your left. Cross over the stile on the far side and continue ahead in the same direction, following the line of the hedge/fence on your left where it curves round to the right near the end of the field. Go diagonally across the following field, on a line between the white cottage to your right and a bungalow nestling in the trees to your left, then through a stile by a gateway and straight ahead with a fence on your right, eventually reaching a lane.

9. Turn right. This broad lane continues for 1¾ miles, giving pleasant open views. You eventually reach Derby Lodge where you turn right. Go up the lane. When you reach a wooden gate on your right, opposite the buildings of Home Farm, leave the road and bear right on to a narrow woodland path. After 100 yards, look to your left to see the mock Tudor building called The Gardens.

The Gardens is a 13-roomed mock Tudor house and was built in 1882, as the dower house of the widow of the late Alfred Miller-Mundy.

In September 1978 Barbara and Geoffrey Cuthbert moved into it. It seems that Barbara had a particular affinity for the house. Seven years earlier she had dreamt she was working in an unfamiliar country house. The dining room of The Gardens proved to be identical to the one in her dream.

Soon after moving in, some strange events took place. Barbara was woken one night by the sound of water pouring out of all the taps in the bathroom. Her husband was unable to turn them off and had to shut it off at the mains. They heard footsteps in their bedroom and at times the bed was violently shaken.

Whenever the porch light was turned off at night, it was always found to have been switched back on. A workman called to repair it saw a figure glide through the closed door.

Barbara and a friend investigated the ghostly phenomenon and found three ghosts connected with the house.

The first was Squire Edward Miller-Mundy, who built the Dower house for his wife. She caused a great scandal by running off with the Earl of Shrewsbury, and though the squire eventually remarried and his body was buried in North London after his death, it seems his spirit remains tied to Shipley Park and the Dower house.

The second ghost is that of John Crago Tallack, who, in 1909, fell down the stairs of the house and broke his ankle. The constant pain from this injury made him suffer months of mental and physical anguish, causing him to sink into despair and depression. Finally, he committed suicide by means of cyanide.

His wife left The Gardens after his death, but it seems her spirit has returned there as she is the third ghost to haunt this fascinating house.

Where the path rejoins the road, keep to the right and continue down the hill back to the car park.

WALK 9
AMBERGATE/ALDERWASLEY

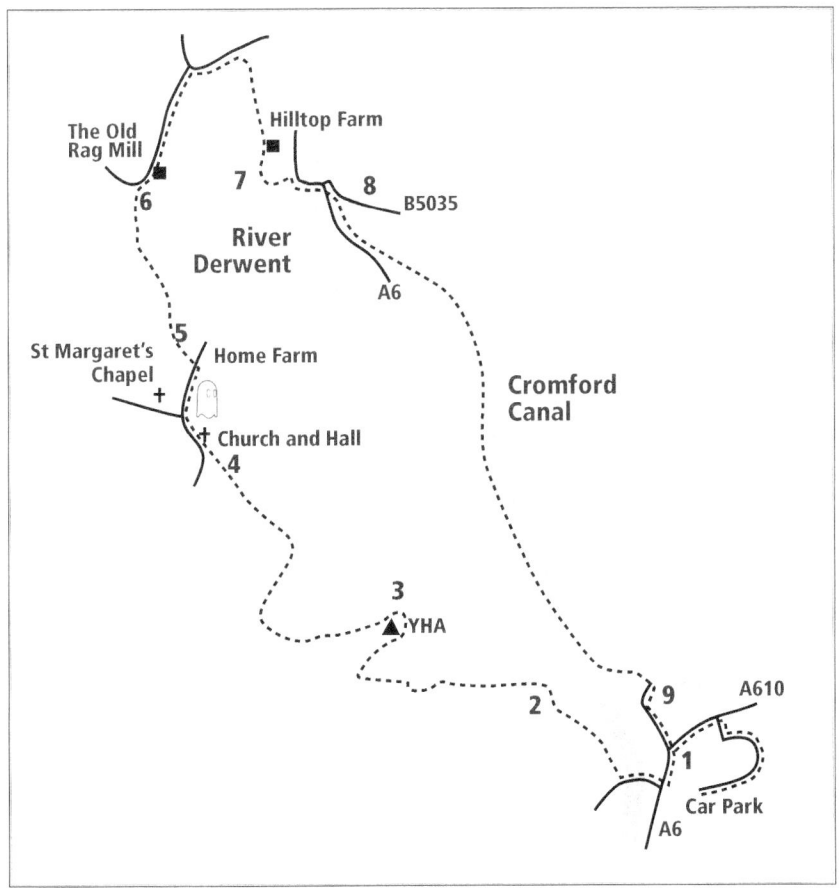

A lovely walk through Birches, Shining Cliff and Beggarswell Woods, made attractive by rhododendrons in May/June and the heady scent of garlic. The first half of this walk involves more energetic climbs but returns with a gentle stroll by the Cromford Canal.

Distance: 7½ miles
Grade: B
Parking: Ambergate Station car park.
Map Ref: SK 349516. Outdoor Leisure Map The White Peak.
Pub Stop: Derwent Arms, Whatstandwell.

Route

1. Leave the car park by the access road and return to the A610. Turn left and left again at the junction with the A6 (opposite the Hurt Arms pub). Cross over the road then turn right when you reach Holly Lane, just before the church. Cross the bridge and where the road forks, turn right by the noticeboard for Alderwasley parish. Go straight ahead into the Birches woodland.

2. At the sign for the YHA, keep left on the broad track. Just after the sign for 'Grith Pioneers', keep straight ahead, ignoring a steep path coming down from the left and staying on the main track. Where the path divides and the main track goes straight on at a second notice board for 'Grith Pioneers',

St Margaret's Chapel, Alderwasley, where you may hear ghostly singing and organ playing.

turn right and go downhill, following a yellow arrow. When you reach the lake at the bottom of the hill, turn right. Cross the stream. When you reach two more notice boards about 'Shining Cliff Woods', turn left at an arrow sign. The path climbs uphill and another arrow directs you to the left.

3. Go past the YHA hostel buildings and continue uphill. When you reach a junction of paths (one to the left followed by one to the right), turn right uphill, off the main track, following the yellow arrow sign. At the top of the rise bear left and follow the path through the trees until you reach a wall and an iron gate to the right (plus a bench for Siward Glaister). Go through the gate, following the sign for 'Midshires Way' and straight down the field with the wall on your right. At the end of the field, go ahead in a green lane between the walls. Cross over the stile next to the iron gate and continue straight ahead on a broad cart track. Where the track bends left, note the wonderfully carved wooden settee in memory of Cyril and Peggy Reynolds.

This is a pleasant spot for a break with a lovely view to enjoy.

Go over a stile by a gate and continue ahead until you eventually reach the road in Alderwasley.

4. Turn right. After a few yards you reach the entrance to Alderwasley Hall and Park.

The church, which is just inside the entrance to the park, is in a beautiful setting and well worth viewing.

The Hurt family who lived at the hall were involved in lead smelting and a legacy of charcoal burning left in connection with this is a fire damaged yew tree known as 'Betty Kenny's Tree'. Every year, Betty Kenny (real name Kate) and her family came to burn charcoal. They camped in a shelter and in good weather the baby was left to sleep outside in the horizontal hollow branch of a tree. It is thought that this is the origin of the nursery rhyme *Rock-a-bye-baby*.

Continue on the road through the village until you reach Chapel Hill on your left. Turn left here to visit St Margaret's Chapel, the site of your ghost story. Go up Chapel Hill, past the notice board for Alderwasley Parish, then, a little further on, turn right into the churchyard. Go down the path to the right, through a gap in the stone wall, and you are then able to visit the chapel by going down the grass bank.

St Margaret's Chapel dates from the 16th century when it was the Hurt family's private chapel. The marble coat of arms (in the wooden glass-fronted frame) presumably belongs to them. The south wall is adorned in carved heads, which came from an earlier building that stood on this sacred site. One or two of them are strange and grotesque and very unchapel-like. There is also said to be a Sheela-na-gig on the left-hand corner, which is a type of medieval pornography, representing the Celtic goddess of creation and destruction. Like gargoyles, they are depicted in horrible forms to frighten away evil spirits. It is, however, very worn and the detail is hard to make out.

The chapel is said to be haunted and local people have told of the sounds of shuffling feet and a doorbell ringing coming from the disused building. Others have heard singing and an organ playing.

There is also a report concerning a hill just past Alderwasley of a 4ft-high figure having been seen wearing a green pointed hat (an elf or fairy?) feeding the plants.

Return to Chapel Hill, turn left then left again at the T junction, following the sign for Whatstandwell and Crich. The road drops down, and at the bottom turn left at the footpath sign (overgrown) by the iron gate, opposite a farm entrance.

5. Go straight ahead on a green lane. Go over a stile at the end and follow the direction of the arrow sign to the right, going down the field with the hedge on your right. Pass through an open gateway, where the path turns left through the next field, with the hedge on your left. Go over a stile and continue straight ahead following the arrow sign in the third field. When you reach the stile at the corner of this field, there is a choice of paths. Go through the gap stile, turning immediately right through a second stile.

Now take the left of two paths, dropping down the field with trees to your left, heading for an attractive house nestled below the evergreen woodland in the distance. NB the monument on Crich Stand is to your right at this point. Go over another stile and head straight down the field, crossing two more stiles and joining a lane.

6. Turn right on the lane past The Old Rag Mill. Continue on this lane until you reach the road, where you turn right. Opposite a house called the Birches, bear right off the road, at a public footpath sign and signs for 'Hilltop Farm' and 'Oakhill Farm'. Keep straight ahead through Hilltop Farm, then where there is a sign for 'Valley View' on the right, go on to a narrow path between hedges marked by a yellow arrow, passing through three gap stiles. Go straight ahead across the next field.

7. Just past the building to your left, turn left following arrows for 'Amber Valley 19 Walk' and 'Derwent Valley Walk'. Go over a stile and bear left down a paved lane. Where the paved track swings right, follow the arrow sign to leave it and go straight ahead. The path then curves sharp right with a wall on your left. Cross straight over a road, over a stile and down the field to emerge on the A6 at Whatstandwell Bridge. Cross the busy road and go over the bridge, past the Derwent Arms Pub and then up the hill on the B5035. The road bends right and then left.

8. Turn right on to the Cromford Canal towpath at the sign for 'Holloway' (which is pointing left). Go under two stone bridges, ignoring the footpath sign to the right by the second. At the third stone bridge, leave the towpath and turn right where arrows for the 'Derwent Valley Walk' and 'Ambergate Station' are marked on the wooden footpath sign.

9. Go right down the lane. Go under the railway bridge and then left at the main A6 road. Turn left at the junction opposite the Hurt Arms, under the bridge, and immediately right up the access road to the Ambergate Station car park.

The Hurt family's Coat of Arms.

WALK 10
AMBERGATE/HEAGE

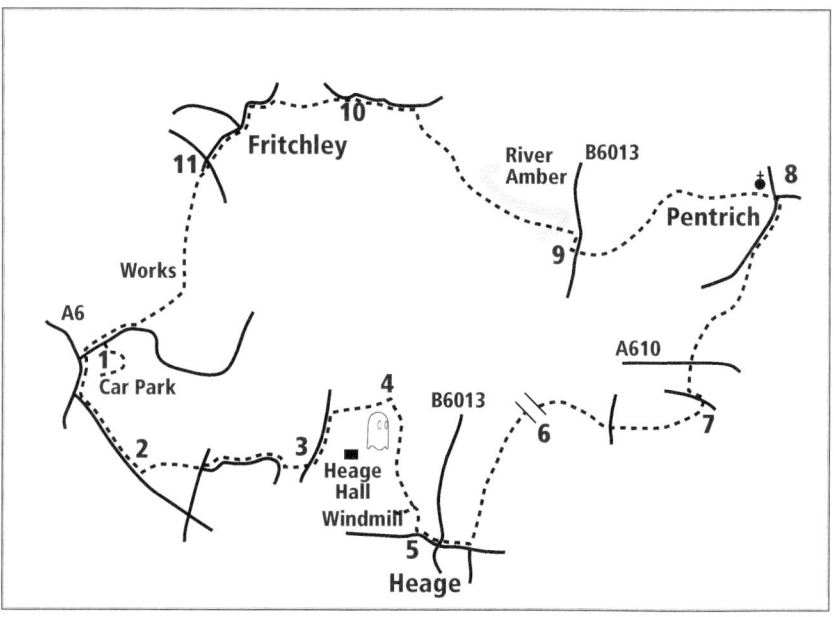

This is a more energetic walk in open countryside with good views throughout. A unique windmill and the chance of an encounter with a ghostly squire coursing his dogs add to the interest of this walk.

Distance:	8 miles
Grade:	B/C
Parking:	Ambergate Station car park.
Map Ref:	SK 349516. Explorer 269 Chesterfield Map.
Pub Stop:	White Hart and Eagle Tavern in Heage after 2½ miles. Dog Inn in Pentrich after 4½ miles. Refreshments may be had at the Corner Café, opposite the Hurt Arms on the A6. It is open on Saturdays, Sundays and Bank Holidays.

Route

1. From the car park return to the A610 road and turn left. Go under the bridge and left again at the T junction on the A6 opposite the Hurt Arms (WCs on the left before the café). After 500 yards, turn left up Newbridge Road, under the bridge and up the hill. Keep straight up, past Toad Moor Lane.

2. When you reach house no.55 on the left, turn left (going back on yourself) on a short cart track past nos.55 and 53 and through a gap stile at the side of no.53, on to a narrow path between the hedge and the wall. Continue into the field with the wall on your left. Cross a track and go down the next field to a stile in the bottom right-hand corner leading on to a lane. Turn left and then immediately right on Nodin Hill Lane. Pass Nodin Hill Farm and continue down the hill, past a lane to the left and on to Gun Lane. Where the road bends to the right at the bottom of the hill, follow the right hand of two public footpath signs. Cross a small field and continue straight ahead in the next one with a hedge on your left and through a further stile to reach a road.

3. Turn left past a row of houses on the right. Continue down the hill, then just before the second row of houses, turn right through a gap stile by a gateway. Cross the first field and continue into the next field, keeping the hedge to your left. Go over the stile in the top corner, to the left of an iron gate, and follow the path in the field with the hedge now on your right.

4. Three quarters of the way up the field, turn right over a stile marked 'Amber Valley 5'. Bear slightly left across the field, passing a small bench to your right (for mounting horses, enjoying the view or an old stile?). Go across a wooden bridge over a stream, bearing left across the corner of the next field to a gap stile. Turn right, following the direction of the arrow with the hedge on your right. Continue ahead on a broad grassy path, up a short rise, to a stile hidden in the hedge into the field beyond.

The stone buildings in the trees in the valley below, to the right, are cottages built on the site of Heage Hall, which was haunted by the ghosts of three former residents.

Heage Hall is haunted by the ghosts of three former residents.

One of the ghosts was that of Mrs Arguile, who committed suicide there. A servant girl called Bessie fainted and died a few weeks later when she saw the deceased Mrs Arguile sitting behind her.

Squire George Pole, who later bought the hall, treated his wife so badly that she too took her own life. As her ghost wandered through the corridors, she was said to look as unhappy and depressed in death as she was in life.

The third ghost was that of George Pole himself, a miser who hoarded his money in a huge oak chest fastened with 12 locks. Although it was guarded closely by him throughout his life, when he died, it was found to be empty.

Charles Shore and his brother later bought Heage Hall and were said to have found the treasure and melted it down. They were frequently woken in the night by a cold hand pressing on their faces, thought to be

George Pole looking for his money. His ghost was also seen in a coach riding through Belper and coursing with his dogs in these fields.

James Black, a smith, encountered his ghost together with two of his spectral dogs, near the church. Black collapsed and died three weeks later.

When Heage Hall was demolished, its stone was used to build the cottages which now stand on its site. The ghosts of Mrs Arguile, Mrs Pole and the Squire are said to still haunt them.

Bear left up the hill to a stile in the corner then on to a track. Your route lies straight across it on 'Amber Valley 5'.

However, you may turn right on the track to visit Heage Windmill, which is worth the short diversion. Built in 1797, it was restored in 2002 and is the only stone-towered, multi-sailed, working windmill in England. It is open April to October, Saturdays, Sundays and Bank holidays, 11am to 4pm.

If you have visited the windmill, return to the point where you reached the track and turn right over a stile marked 'Amber Valley 5'. Go diagonally left across the field. Cross a stile leading on to a path between a fence and hedge, keeping straight ahead over three more stiles until you reach the road.

5. Turn left into Heage.

One dark night in September 1842 three men from Heage, John Hulme, William Bland and Samuel Bonsall, robbed a house at Stanley Common. They beat the owners: two spinsters, Sarah and Martha Goddard. Sarah survived, but unfortunately Martha died. The three were caught and hanged, giving rise to the local saying 'They hang them in bunches in Heage,' and 'You can tell a man from Heage by the rope burns on his neck.'

At the T junction at the end turn left, crossing the B6013, signposted 'Heage Windmill', past the White Hart pub (or go in; it's open all day/Sunday lunches) and go down Eagle Street. Just before the Eagle Tavern (another pub stop?) opposite Brook Street, turn left on to Bond Lane. Go along a track and past Bond Lane Farm and continue ahead on to a green lane. At the end of the lane, go over a stile and down a field with the hedge on your right. Go through an open gateway, passing a farm on your left, then on to a track. After 100 yards, when the track bends right, go over a stile by a gate, passing the large pond, to Starvehimvalley Bridge.

There doesn't seem to be any information available to explain this unusual and fascinating name. However, many tenant farmers named their plots with wry humour, examples being Bare Bottoms in Outseats, Back Break Meadow in Smerrill, Sour Lands at Great Hucklow and a number of Hungry Hills in the county, making it clear what they thought of their holdings. One can only assume that Starvehimvalley was named in the same manner.

6. Go over the bridge and turn immediately right before the stile (i.e. not on the path straight ahead) to walk with the water on your right. Go ahead in the field with the hedge on your left-hand side. Where the hedge bends left, bear right across the field to a stile and walk in the same direction in the following field. Cross the stile on the far side, past some houses on your right. Go over the next stile, with some cottages on your left, to reach a road. Cross the road and go straight ahead through a narrow paddock and on to a paved path beside an old canal.

7. When you reach a bridge, go up the slope at the side of it then turn left and cross the road. Turn right at the footpath sign and immediately bear left along a path across the field to emerge on the A610 road beside a bus shelter. Cross this very busy and fast road with care. Turn right then left after 20 yards at a footpath sign hidden in the hedge, just before reaching the bus shelter on this side. This leads to a narrow footpath between hedges. Go along this footpath and also the following cart track, ignoring a

footpath sign on the right between some buildings, continuing until you reach Wood Lane in Pentrich, where you turn right. When you reach the Dog Inn, bear left at the road junction and left again at the public footpath sign to 'Pentrich Mill'.

Note the plaque on the wall: 'Pentrich Revolution June 9th 1817 St Matthews Church'. The curate hid rebels here from the government troops.

8. Go up the steps into the churchyard and through a stile in the top-left corner into the field and continue straight ahead in the direction of the arrow. Cross over a stile on the far side of the field and follow the direction of the left-hand arrow sign. Go through a gap stile and, following the direction of another arrow, turn right, walking with the hedge and electricity pylon on right. Go over the stile at the end of this field and turn left, now walking with the hedge on your left in this field and the following two fields. In the third field, follow the line of the hedge round to the right, dropping down the hill, through a small wooden gate to reach a road opposite an old mill (B6013).

Note the plaque on the side of the mill: 'Pentrich Revolution June 9th 1817. Booth's Hovel. Hiding place of Thomas Bacon was near here'.

9. Turn right and then left at a footpath sign. Cross the bridge over the River Amber and ahead on the footpath with the river on your right-hand side. (NB you are between a loop of the river at this point so there is river on both sides!) Stay close to the river on your right on a little used path (overgrown in summer). The path eventually starts to climb and emerges on to a cart track. Continue uphill, through the farmyard and straight ahead on the lane. Drop down the hill. At the bottom you pass tracks to the left and right, gated with 'No Admittance' on them. Then, where the lane bends to the right, go left over the stile and follow the direction of the arrow to the right. In the next field bear right, again following the arrow sign. Go over a stile on to a lane where you turn left.

10. Continue until you reach a sign for 'Wingfield Park Farm' on the left. Leave the road over a stile and go diagonally across the field to a gap in the hedge on the far side, 30 yards from the top of the field. Continue in the same direction in the following field. Cross over the stile on the far side of the field where you have a choice of paths. Take the one going straight on, where you walk with a hedge on your right. After 100 yards turn right through a gateway (arrow signs are hidden on gateposts in the hedge). Go diagonally left down the field, heading towards the bottom corner. The stile is 20 yards to the right of this. Go on to the lane and turn left into the village of Fritchley. Stay on the main road, passing the village green and a telephone box on your right, going on to Allen Lane.

11. When you reach a T junction, go straight over on to a broad path signposted 'Public Footpath to Ambergate'. Go through a stile, then where the path divides (at an iron gate) go left, dropping downhill. Keep straight down, ignoring any paths off, continuing with a chain-link fence to your left and works to your right. The path winds, passes alongside the railway and eventually emerges on to the A610 road. Turn right then left before the railway bridge, to go back up the access road to the station car park.

WALK 11
MAPLETON LANE, NEAR ASHBOURNE

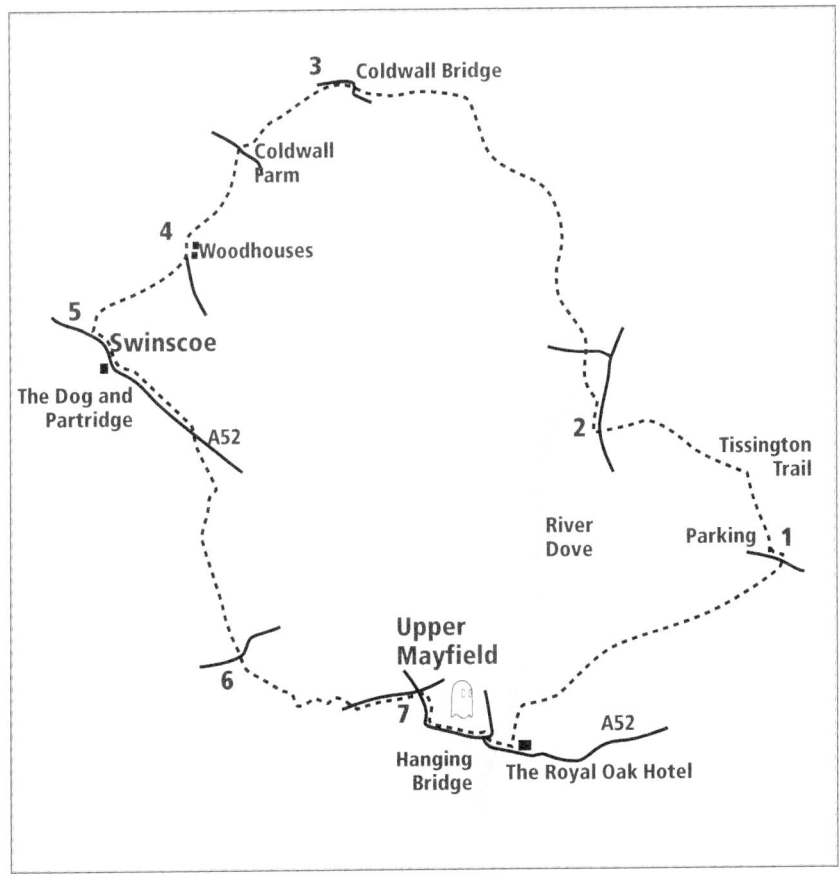

This is a lovely walk to the east of Ashbourne, taking in a quiet part of the River Dove, where a kingfisher may be seen, with panoramic views in undulating terrain.

NB some paths may be overgrown in midsummer.

Distance: 8½ miles

Grade: B/C

Parking: From Ashbourne market place, follow the signs for the 'Tissington Trail' to the car park at Mapleton Lane.

Map Ref: SK 175470. Explorer 259 Derby Map.

Pub Stop: The Dog and Partridge Country Inn at Swinscoe (although this is a bit upmarket for walkers with muddy boots and is expensive).

The Royal Oak Hotel after the Hanging Bridge, reached after 7 miles, is more welcoming and has a large beer garden.

Route

1. From the car park go past reception and the cycle hire shop on to the Tissington Trail. Go ahead on the trail, going down a hill, over a bridge and up the other side. Pass through the gate at the top then turn left down a flight of steps off the trail. Go over the stile and follow the arrow sign up the field. Cross the stile at the top and continue in the same direction in the following field. Go over a stile by a gate and continue ahead along a cart track. Halfway down the field, turn right through a gateway and then turn left. Where the track forks, take the one to the right through the campsite to reach a double stile in the bottom right-hand corner. Bear right across the field then walk adjacent to the right-hand hedge in the following one. There are lovely views to the right of the hills of Dovedale at this point. Halfway down the field, go through the gap in the hedge and continue down, with the hedge now on your left, to reach a gap stile at the bottom. Continue in the same direction to another stile leading on to a drive and to the road.

2. Cross over the road and turn right along the pavement. When you reach a house on your left, turn left over a stile at a public footpath sign. Follow the direction of the sign, heading diagonally across the field to a stile in the corner. Go ahead with the River Dove on your left. As you near a bridge over the river, the path veers to the right to a stile in the middle of the wall. Cross the road and go through a stile on the far side and continue ahead. Pass through two fields adjacent to the river, then, in the third field, the path bears right to a gap in the middle of the far hedge. At the end of the following field the path goes over a small wooden bridge and rejoins the river. Continue on this path, ignoring a path to the right after about ¾ mile.

Kingfishers may be seen on this part of the river.

When you reach a stile with a sign 'Footpath' along the fence, proceed with the fence on your right. Go past a building on your right with a large sign for 'PATH' and continue on a cart track. Go through a gap stile by a gate and up the hill to Coldwall Bridge.

This was where the Thorpe to Blythe turnpike crossed the River Dove at the Derbyshire/Staffordshire boundary. It was known as the old 'Coal Road'.

3. Go straight over the bridge. Where the track starts to rise, ignore footpaths to the right and left and go ahead over a stile by a wooden gate, following the direction of the arrow for the Limestone Way. Climb up the field to the top left-hand corner to the gate (i.e. not to the stile to the right of this). Go through the gate and on to the lane beyond. Pass through Coldwall Farm, continuing on the lane until you reach the road. Go straight over through the gap stile on the far side. Follow the direction of the arrow, bearing right in this field in line with the grey buildings on the hillside opposite and eventually dropping down to a gap in the bottom right-hand corner. Go up the field in the same directions but keeping the buildings slightly to your left to reach a gate on to a lane.

4. Turn left. Ignore a footpath sign to the right. Go through a wooden gate and pass the farmhouse, then, just before the smaller barn on the left, turn right over a stile in the fence on your right. Bear left up the field to a gap stile 50 yards from the top left-hand corner. Go straight across the following field towards a small barn. With the barn to your left, go over a stile, across a small field and through a gap with a broken gate (at the time of writing). Bear right, cutting across the corner of the field and through a gap in the wall. In the following field, go diagonally left to the top corner of the field (opposite end to the farm) to a stile between the telegraph poles. Bear left down the next field and cross under the telephone wires to a stile hidden in the hedge, 30 yards to the left of the farm track, close to the left-hand stone wall.

5. On the road (A52) turn left. The Dog and Partridge Country Inn is on the right. After leaving the pub, cross over to the pavement and turn right to continue in the same direction as before. Where the pavement ends, cross back to the other side (at the house called Hill Crest). Pass the 50 limit sign and the public bridleway at the sign for 'New House Farm'. Where the road bends left, just before another 50 limit sign, turn right on to a public footpath, over a stile and into a field. Bear left, cutting across the left-hand corner, to the second iron gate from the left. Follow the direction of the arrows down the next field with the hedge on your left. At the bottom of the field, do not go over the stile, but turn right along the bottom hedge to a stile hiding in the right-hand corner. In the next field, remain adjacent to the hedge on your left. At the bottom of the field, do not go through the gate but move 20 yards to your right, to a stile hidden in the hedge. Go down the next two fields with the hedge on your left. Cross over the stile at the end of the second field and bear right in the third to a stile by the far right-hand corner. In the fourth field, proceed with the hedge on your right. Go through a stile by a gateway, with a farm to your left (called Lordspiece). Continue with the hedge on your right, but where it ends, bear left to a stile by the gatepost and on to the road (Stanton Lane).

6. Go straight across the road, over the stile by a gate and down a green lane. At the end of the green lane, turn right and immediately left through a gap stile and immediately left again through a gap stile in the hedge ahead. Go diagonally across the field, heading for the second telegraph pole from the left to a gap stile in the hedge.

I have often wondered why holly should be planted at so many stiles, having forced my way through it and endured its prickles over many years. There is a great deal of folklore attached to it. Like many native

trees, it was felt to have protective qualities and there were taboos against cutting it down, which is why it may be left untrimmed. A more practical reason is that farmers may use its distinctive evergreen shape to establish lines of sight for winter ploughing. It is said to guard against lightning, poisoning and mischievous spirits. My favourite explanation is that it stops witches from running along the tops of hedges, so be thankful for this the next time you are being scratched!

Continue diagonally across the following field to a stile in the corner. Bear slightly left down a hill to a stile 50 yards from the right-hand corner. Cross over the stile and down to the paved lane where you turn left. Go down to a kissing gate at the side of an electronic gate and continue ahead on a stony track. Keep ahead on a lane through the houses of Upper Mayfield until you reach a crossroads.

7. At the crossroads, turn right, then where the road forks take the left one with the 'no entry' signs. When you reach the road at the bottom, continue ahead then turn right on the A52 over Hanging Bridge.

Hanging Bridge, Ashbourne, is guarded by a terrifying headless phantom.

The bridge is thought to be the former site of a gallows and is haunted by two ghosts. A headless phantom stands on the bridge late at night, terrifying anyone crossing it. The other is the ghost of a man who jumps off the bridge into the shallow river.

8. Just before The Royal Oak Hotel, turn left at a public footpath sign along a lane. Where the lane swings right towards the car park, turn left, walking alongside an iron fence, and cross a stile by a wooden gate. Go straight ahead across the next three fields, going over the stile at the end of the third, then climb on to the top of the flood bank and turn right along it. After 200 yards, go over a stile, then 50 yards further on leave the flood bank and turn left over another stile. Cross the field diagonally to another stile with a stream on your left. As you emerge into the field, bear right to where the right-hand hedge protrudes into the field. Keep going straight ahead, parallel to the hedge on your right, to a stile in the middle of the hedge/fence at the far end.

Continue straight ahead in the next field with the hedge on your left. When you reach an iron gate, turn right up a hill. Continue for 20 yards with the hedge on your left, then turn left over a stile. Bear right up to the top of the field (but not over the stile at the top) then contour round to the left, staying at the top of the next three fields.

The attractive building on the opposite hillside is the Callow Hall Country House Hotel. It is an early Victorian country house built in around 1840–50 in Elizabethan style. It is a small, 16-bedroom, family-run hotel with roaring log fires and four-poster beds. It is in the *Good Food Guide* and is recommended for its imaginative modern English food.

Pass through a stile in the corner of the last field and continue along a narrow path between the hedges to reach a road. Turn left and then right, back into the car park.

WALK 12
BELPER

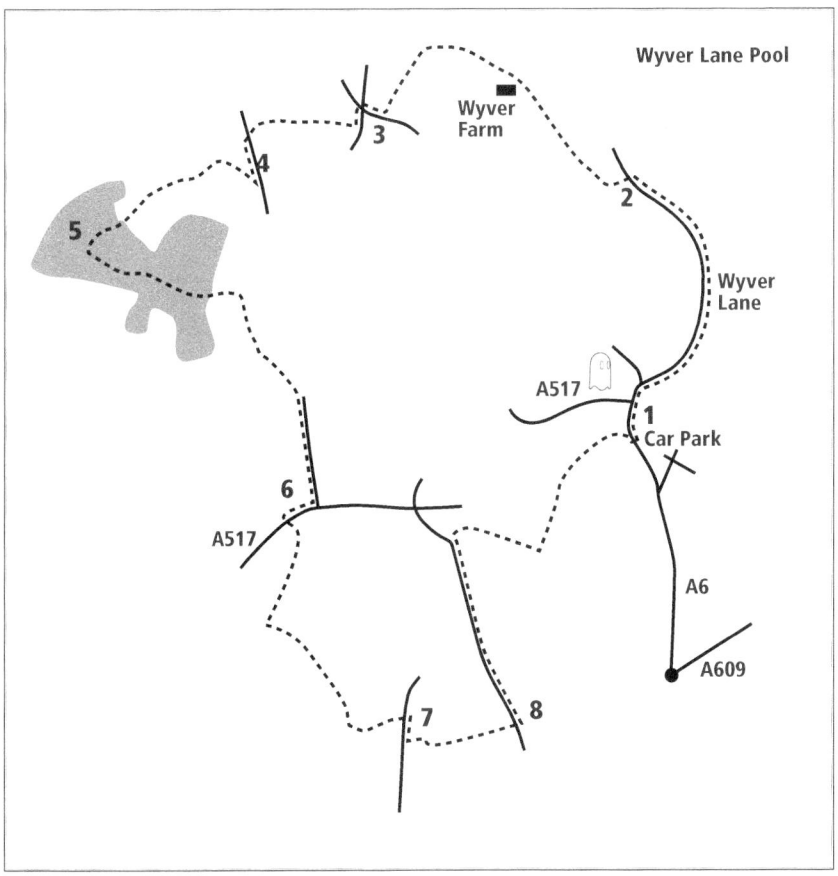

This is a pleasant undulating walk (with two steep hills!) to the north west of Belper, mostly on good paths and tracks, taking you through a variety of fields and woodland. However, it can be muddy in winter. It has open views and a mysterious faceless horseman adds ghostly interest.

Distance: 6 miles
Grade: A/B
Parking: Derwent Valley Visitors' Centre on A517 in Belper. NB parking is limited and car park can be busy at weekends.
Map Ref: SK 345481. Explorer 259 Derby Map.
Pub Stop: Bluebell Inn at Farnah Green (after 4½ miles).

Route

1. Leave the car park by the entrance and turn right on to the road, crossing the bridge over the River Derwent. Where the main road goes left, turn right following the sign for Belper Lane End and Alderwasley. After 30 yards, bear right on to Wyver Lane, passing some very attractive cottages. Continue on the lane for just over ½ mile, ignoring a footpath on the left.

2. Then, just after a notice board for 'Wyver Lane Pool' (an interesting spot for water birds), turn left through a gate at a sign for 'public bridleway' and 'Wyver Farm', going ahead on a track. Stay on the track across the fields then through a gate into Wyver Farm. Go straight through the farmyard, through two gates, following the green arrows for 'Amber Valley Routeway'. Cross three fields with the wall on your right, continuing ahead until you reach a road.

3. Turn right then left at the main road at the Bull's Head pub. After 50 yards (just before the telephone box), turn right at public footpath sign on Jesse's Lane. Go straight ahead into a field, where you walk up the steep hill, with a wall on your right. At the top, go over the stile into woodland and go straight through the wood. Leaving the wood, go straight across the field on to a lane, where you turn left. Where the track forks, turn sharp right at the bridleway sign.

4. Where the track curves to the right, leave it and go straight ahead through an iron gate (not through one to your left). Leave the cart track and, walking with the hedge on your right, head for a house to be seen in the trees. Rejoin the cart track at the bottom, turning right through the gate. Go between the house on your right and outhouse to the left to a yellow arrow sign. Follow a narrow path as it curves left down the field (overgrown with nettles in summer). At the bottom, go left before the wall then after 30 yards go right through gap into the next field. Bear left to a gap in the wall. Go straight across five fields then through a stile by a gate into the wood.

5. After 100 yards, turn left on to a path. Ignore a path to the right after another 300 yards. Continue through the wood, eventually climbing up steeply and emerging into a field. Cross two fields. Go through the stile at the end of the second and turn right and then right through a gap stile to go down a field with a wall on your right. Bear slightly left at the bottom of the field to go through a gap stile by the side of the fencing. Go straight ahead on the cart track, continuing down two fields, through an iron gate on to a stony lane. Turn right and remain on the lane, ignoring paths to the left and right, continuing down to a main road (A517).

6. Turn right. When you reach the telephone box, turn left on to a public bridleway, past the ford. Pass houses to the left and right, then 100 yards further on turn left through a gap stile marked 'Midshires Way'. Cross a small field, then in the next go diagonally left, up a large field to a wood. Go into the woodland, staying on the path, until you emerge into a field. Go straight ahead with the wall on your left. When you reach a lane, cross over to a stile on the other side, following signs for 'Midshires Way'. Go down the lane to reach a road.

7. Turn right. After 50 yards you will reach a public bridleway sign, where you turn left. However, there is a pub, the Bluebell, 100 yards further down this road for those in need of refreshment. Go ahead on the bridleway. Where it turns to the right (at a bench for the Spencer Family), turn left following the yellow arrow sign for the 'Derwent Valley Walk' (leaving Midshires Way). Go down two fields to reach a road.

8. Turn left. Ignore two public footpaths to the right then drop down the hill to reach a public footpath on the right, which is your route. However, to visit the scene of the haunted crossroads, continue down the lane for a short distance, passing a junction where Farnah Green comes in from the left towards the crossroads with the main A517.

In August 1992, at 11.30am, Mike Woodhouse was travelling on this road towards these crossroads. He saw a rider on a horse dressed in black and wearing a three-cornered hat and cloak. The black horse was standing outside the old coachhouse and stables on the left side of the junction from where you are standing. Mike glanced away to check for traffic, and when he looked back the horse and rider had disappeared. Although he checked all the roads, he found no sign of them.

Two weeks later he approached the same junction at 5.30am from the opposite direction. He again saw the rider, but this time realised that he was faceless; there was a black space where his face should have been. This was upsetting enough, but in addition the horseman disappeared while he was looking at him! Three weeks later at 6am the same scene occurred, with horse and rider vanishing as he watched. Shaken by these events, Mike changed his route after this. He has returned since with his wife, who was anxious to see the phantom horseman, but they have had not succeeded so far. Perhaps you will be luckier!

Farnah Green, Belper, where a mysterious faceless horseman may appear.

Return to the public footpath and go down the lane. Keep straight ahead, ignoring a lane to the left. After ¼ mile, look for a footpath to the left with 'NO CYLING' on it in large letters. (If you reach some iron gates you have come too far and should retrace your steps by 50 yards.) Cross two fields, continuing on to a paved lane to eventually reach the main A517 road. Turn right back to the visitors' centre.

WALK 13
HAZELWOOD

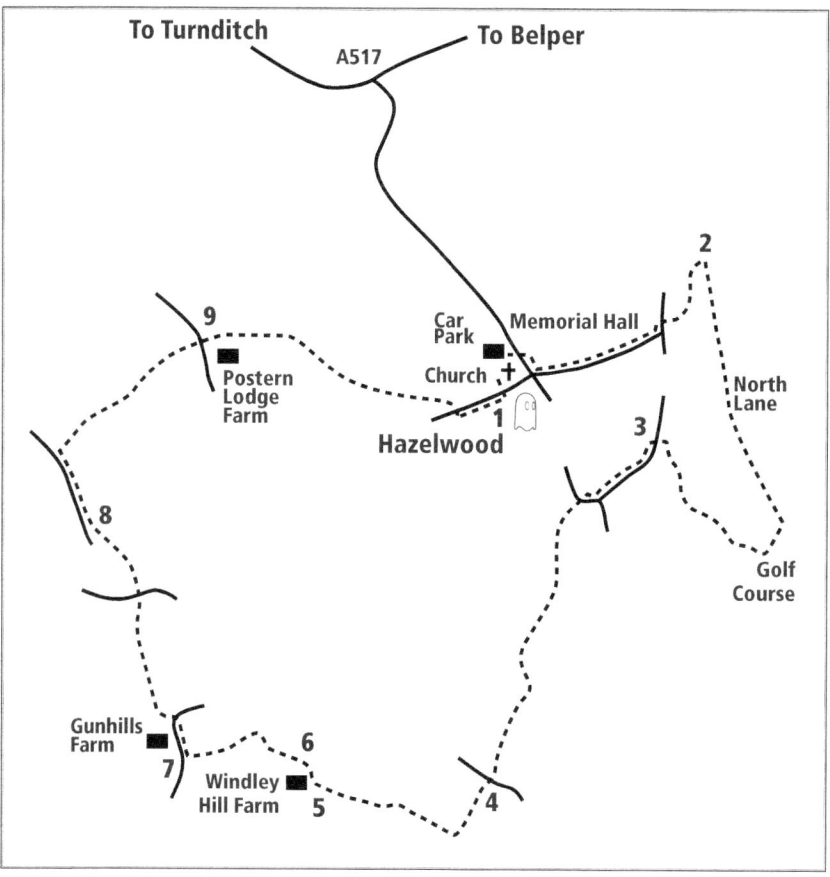

This is an undulating walk with extensive views in an area to the south west of Belper.

NB some paths and stiles may be overgrown in summer, and it is recommended that you do this walk in spring, autumn or winter or take a machete for the nettles!

Distance: 7½ miles

Grade: B

Parking: Memorial Hall car park (next to church) on Over Lane, which leads from A517 to Hazelwood. There is additional car parking in an adjacent field.

Map Ref: SK 328461. Explorer 259 Derby Map.

Pub Stop: None.

Route

1. Leave the car park by the entrance and turn right on the road. At the crossroads, turn left following signs for Farnah Green and Belper on Goodwins Lane. Stay on this road for ½ mile until you reach a T junction. Turn left, then after 30 yards turn right at a footpath sign. Go ahead up a narrow path, following the yellow arrow sign at a junction. At the top of the rise where you see a stone wall ahead, follow the yellow arrow sign to the left. Continue to follow the yellow arrows on a pleasant, wide woodland path, which eventually drops down between the walls to a T junction.

2. Turn right on a broad track (North Lane). Stay on this track for ¾ mile but look out for gates to the right and left, with signs saying 'Private Land' on them and access to the golf course. Fifty yards after this, turn right at a yellow footpath sign marked 'Derwent Valley Walk' (Chevinend on map). Go down between the fence and the wall. Cross two access paths for the golf course and continue down, following the yellow arrow signs. When you reach a wall, do not go over it, but turn right, walking with the wall on your left (note there is no arrow sign for this path). When the path ends, continue on to a track, through the buildings and on to a lane.

3. Turn left. After 50 yards note the Hazelwood Spring on the right, which has never been known to fail. At the road junction, turn right towards Hazelwood and Shottlegate. After 50 yards turn left on an unmarked lane with a mirror on its left hand side and black and white chevrons. When you reach an old barn/garage, turn left down a green lane. Go right at the fork. When you reach the field, follow the sign for 'Amber Valley Routeways 10'. Go down two fields with the hedge on your left. Go over the stile at the bottom of the second field, cross the track, then go left over two stiles and follow the direction of the arrow, to walk with the hedge on your right in a third field. In the following field, bear slightly left to the stile in the top left-hand corner. Cross the railway line and the next field with the hedge on your left. At the end, bear left over a stile and round to the right. Cross the bridge over the River Ecclesbourne and bear slightly left across the field (not on 'Amber Valley Routeways 10') to a stile by the telegraph pole. Continue straight ahead, with the hedge on your left, to the road.

4. Turn right and immediately left before the house (Farnah Lodge). Go through the gate and on to a broad green track. After 500 yards, when you reach the edge of the wood, and three yellow arrow signs, turn right (note there is no arrow for this direction). Go over the stile and ahead along two fields with the hedge on your right. Continue in a third field, now with the hedge on your left, at the end of which you will reach a track and some derelict buildings.

5. The designated footpath goes left through the buildings then follows a yellow arrow sign on a gate directing you to the right. You go over a stile and through undergrowth with a fence on your left and then turn left at the top. However, this path may be completely overgrown with nettles, particularly in summer, and so may be almost impassable. An alternative from the track is to go right for about 10 yards then left up the uneven field, heading for the fence on the horizon, but note this is not on a footpath.

6. Having reached the fence by whichever means, you then proceed with it on your left-hand side. Go through three gateways, then, after 30 yards, turn left following the yellow arrow and then over a stile on the right. Follow the direction of the yellow arrow across a field. Go through an open gateway, bearing right in a second field towards the copse on the hill. Continue in the same direction in the following field to a stile in the corner. Go ahead with the fence on your left to reach a lane.

7. Turn right. Pass Gunhills Farm then turn left at a public footpath sign, up the steps. Bear right in the field heading for the right hand one of the line of trees. Cross the next small field then go down the centre of the following

St John the Evangelist, Hazelwood, is haunted by a sad weeping girl.

one, bearing right to the stile in the bottom right corner on to a lane. Cross the lane and go over the stile on the far side. Bear right to the footbridge then bear left in a field to a gateway halfway along a hedge. In the following field, go diagonally right, heading for the stile 20 yards from the top corner and a footpath by the side of the modern bungalow to the road.

8. Turn right and follow the road uphill. Just before the top of the hill, turn right at a public footpath sign along a drive leading to The Green. Turn left through an iron gate, following the yellow marker, and walk round with the house on your right. Go through a second gateway and follow the yellow marker along the field with the hedge to your right. At the end of the field, go through a stile (behind the open gate) and continue in the same direction, still keeping the hedge to your right, passing through a gap in the bottom hedge to reach the next field. At the end of this field, turn left, following a fence on your right to reach a double stile after 100 yards. Cross this double stile and walk, with a hedge now on your left, towards a stile by an iron gate. Go over this stile, through a second iron gate, over the disused railway line and along the lane to reach the road.

9. Go straight over to Postern Lodge Farm and bear left over a stile by an iron gate. Follow the direction of the arrow signs, bearing right in the field. Continue over a stile and ahead with the fence on your right. Bear right down the next field to a stile in the bottom corner (not through the gateway on the left). Go over another stile and continue ahead with the hedge on your left. On the far side, follow the direction of the yellow arrow sign through an open gateway, then go diagonally across the field to a stile in the top left-hand corner. Continue in the same direction in the following field, going towards the buildings to be seen in the distance. On the far side of the field bear right, keeping above the hollow to an awkward stile, well hidden in the right-hand hedge, 10 yards before the corner. Turn left and keep the hedge on your left for two fields. In the second field, look for a stile again hidden in the hedge, about 50 yards from the top right-hand corner. Go over a stile and turn right to reach the road. Turn left and go up the hill to the village, passing the Church of St John the Evangelist.

There are a number of reported sightings of a ghost seen in the churchyard.

One was from a photographer from the local newspaper, attending a celebration party at the village hall for the Queen's Silver Jubilee in 1998. The car park was full so he parked by the wall of the church behind the car of Peter and Carol Booth.

Peter noticed the photographer staring into the churchyard with a strange expression on his face.

When Peter jokingly asked him if he'd seen a ghost, he replied, 'I'm sure I have.' He went on to describe a young woman in a white dress with buttons down the back and lovely auburn hair. She was kneeling with her arm on a gravestone and resting her forehead on her arm.

Talking to other villagers, Peter discovered that the ghost had been seen frequently, including by two ladies at a funeral who had fainted because of it.

Many years later, Peter's sister Gwen told the story to her son's girlfriend Ruth when they drove past the churchyard. Ruth became very quiet and Gwen interpreted this as scepticism from the very down to earth computer analyst. She was therefore surprised when Gwen admitted that she too had seen the girl, weeping and holding a posy of flowers to her chest. She had found the girl's distress so sad that she had felt compelled to look away. When she glanced back the girl had disappeared.

Ruth had no idea of the other stories about the ghost and had not discussed the incident with anyone.

Continue to the crossroads where you turn left and then left again back into the car park.

WALK 14
SWARKESTONE BRIDGE

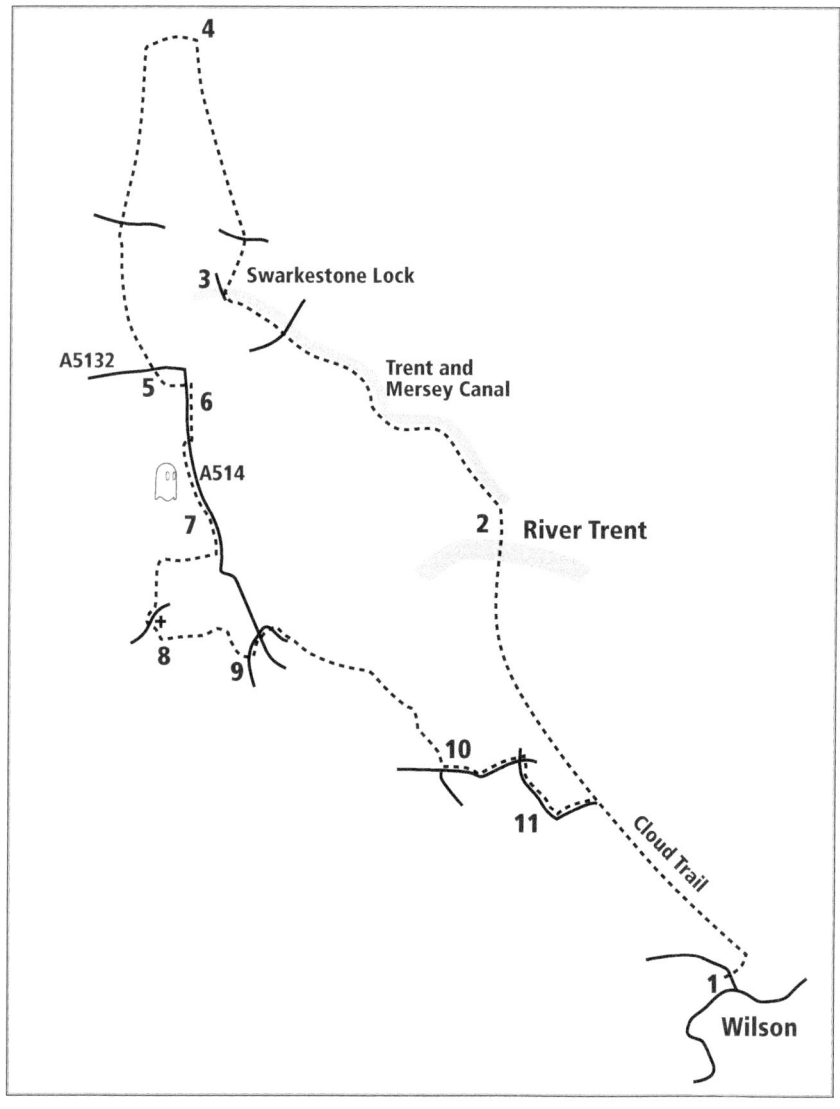

This is a flat easy 10-mile walk mostly on good tracks and trails in an area to the north and east of Melbourne. The fascinating history of the 14th-century Swarkestone Bridge with its ghostly associations adds to its interest.

Distance: 10 miles

Grade: A

Parking: Limited parking in a lay-by opposite the start of the Cloud Trail in Wilson. Some additional street parking may be found in the village.

Map Ref: SK 404248. Explorer 245 The National Forest and Explorer 259 Derby Maps.

Pub Stop: The Crewe and Harpur at Swarkestone Bridge has a good range of beers and lagers and serves sandwiches, snacks and main meals with tea or coffee.

Route

1. From the lay-by, cross the road bearing left then go immediately right at the sign for the 'Cloud Trail', along a stony track. When you reach a bridge, turn left at a sign for the 'Cloud Trail'. Go down the slope and follow the sign for Melbourne and Derby. When you reach a junction of paths, continue straight ahead following the sign for Derby. Stay on the trail for another ½ mile. Cross the bridge over the River Trent and carry on until you reach another bridge (Sarsons Bridge) and a junction of paths.

2. Turn left down the hill to reach the Trent and Mersey Canal and left again to walk with the canal on your right, continuing on the towpath for 1½ miles until you reach Swarkestone Lock.

3. Turn right over the brick bridge. Go on to the paved lane and follow this lane round a right-hand bend, along the pathway following the sign for Derby, walking with the disused Derby Canal on your left. Pass under the busy A50 road. The path curves right, crosses a bridge and left again. Continue until you reach a junction of paths (about ¾ mile from the A50).

4. Turn left following the sign for Sinfin. Ignore a footpath to the right, staying on the trail. Cross a bridge over a small stream then, at the end of

Swarkestone Bridge is haunted by two bereft sisters and the sounds of Bonnie Prince Charlie's troops.

the field on your left, turn left on a stony lane to walk with the hedge on your right. Keep ahead where the stony track becomes a paved road and cross the bridge over the A50. In just under ½ mile you cross over the Trent and Mersey Canal, which provides a possible picnic spot by the canal side. Go across a bridge over a railway and continue until you reach a main road (A5132).

5. Cross straight over on to Wood Shop Lane. Stay on the lane as it curves round to the left to reach another main road, the A514, and a pub, the Crewe and Harpur.

The pub has lots of picnic tables leading down to the river and serves a good range of beers and lagers as well as sandwiches and main meals with tea or coffee.

6. Turn right on the A514 and cross Swarkestone Bridge over the River Trent. Continue on the narrow footpath on the right-hand side of the road for about 100 yards. As the path becomes very narrow, you reach some railings. Go right here, either down the stone steps (if not barricaded by a palette by the farmer) or through the railings into the field and turn left. You can admire this amazing structure on your left-hand side as you walk beside it.

Swarkestone Bridge, which crosses the River Trent and low-lying marshland, is almost a mile in length and is the longest stone bridge in England. It was built in the early 13th century as the result of a tragic love story.

When two sisters of the Bellamont family became betrothed, they decided to celebrate. On the day of the party, their fiancés had to attend a meeting with the barons on the far side of the River Trent, and while they were there, a storm caused the river to become swollen. Anxious to return to the celebrations and their beautiful women, the men attempted to ford the river on horseback but were swept away by the torrent and drowned.

The Bellamont girls built the bridge over the Trent to prevent anyone

else suffering the same tragedy. They never married and died in poverty, having spent so much money on the bridge. Observing the length of its construction, one can see why.

Their ghosts are said to haunt it on stormy nights, searching the raging river for their lost loves.

There is also said to be a water elemental that requires three lives per year to remain pacified, so take care as you cross, as I don't know what its tally is for this year!

In 1745 Swarkestone Bridge was the furthest point south reached by Bonnie Prince Charlie's troops. As it was the only means of crossing the River Trent between Nottingham and Burton, on 4 December 70 troops were sent to secure it.

Over the years, there have been many strange happenings associated with the bridge. A typical one is that of a man walking his dog one night, who heard the clatter of horses' hooves and talking becoming louder and louder. He waited in vain for the riders to appear and says that when the noise was at its loudest it suddenly stopped.

A number of people have reported the same experience. Could it be that they are hearing the echoes of the troops of Bonnie Prince Charlie from all those years ago?

7. Go over a stile and keep straight ahead. Cross a second stile and continue to the end of the field, then turn right through an iron gate with an arrow sign. Pass through a second gate and walk straight ahead, following the yellow sign when passing the farm. Turn left following the direction of the next arrow on a telegraph pole, going up the field with the fence on your left. Go diagonally right across the field at the top and over a stile by the side of an iron gate, down a short green lane to the road.

8. Turn right, then, just past the church, turn left at the public footpath sign. Go up a stony lane which winds left and then right. At the end of the houses, just after the public footpath sign, turn left, walking with the hedge on your left. Where the hedge turns left, follow it round for a few yards and then go right at the footpath sign, under the bar of a stile (a chance to practice your limbo dancing!) on to a narrow path (overgrown in summer). Go straight ahead over the next two fields, then into the paddock of the attractive house. Just before the gate at the bottom, go right over a stile and left on the lane. At the T junction, turn right and continue ahead.

9. When you reach the main road, cross over and turn left to reach a junction. Cross over, bearing slightly right, and go down a narrow paved lane. After 30 yards, turn right over a stile and up the field, bearing right at the top and over a stile in the corner. Turn left to walk with the wood on your left. In the field, head for the electricity pylon to reach a stile at the back of it, leading to a cart track. Turn right. You continue straight on along this track for about a mile until you reach the road.

On the latter part there is a sign for a Holy Well, which you may visit by descending a few steps.

The earliest documentary evidence of the Holy Well was in 1366 when the spring and stream were referred to as Halywalsiche. The inscription roughly translates as 'This Holy Well was built by Robert named Hardinge 1662.' Although the quality of the water was said to be excellent, there is no evidence that the well was particularly renowned for its healing qualities.

In 1978 the well was just a muddy brook and a pile of stones. However, thanks to the efforts of the Melbourne Civic Society, over many years, the well's restoration was finally completed in 1985.

10. Turn left opposite Ye Old Pack Horse Pub along Main Street. Pass a second pub, the Hardinge Arms. Continue until you reach the war memorial, where you turn right. Where the road bends to the right, leave it, going straight ahead following a footpath sign across the field. Go between the houses to reach the road.

11. Turn left. Pass a road to the left then turn right at a bridge on to the Cloud Trail. Stay on the trail for a mile then just after a bridge over the trail, where the trail forks, go right following the sign for the 'Bulls Head'. At the top of the rise, turn right on a stony lane, staying on it to reach the main road. Turn left to parking.

Walk 15 and 16
HOLMEWOOD

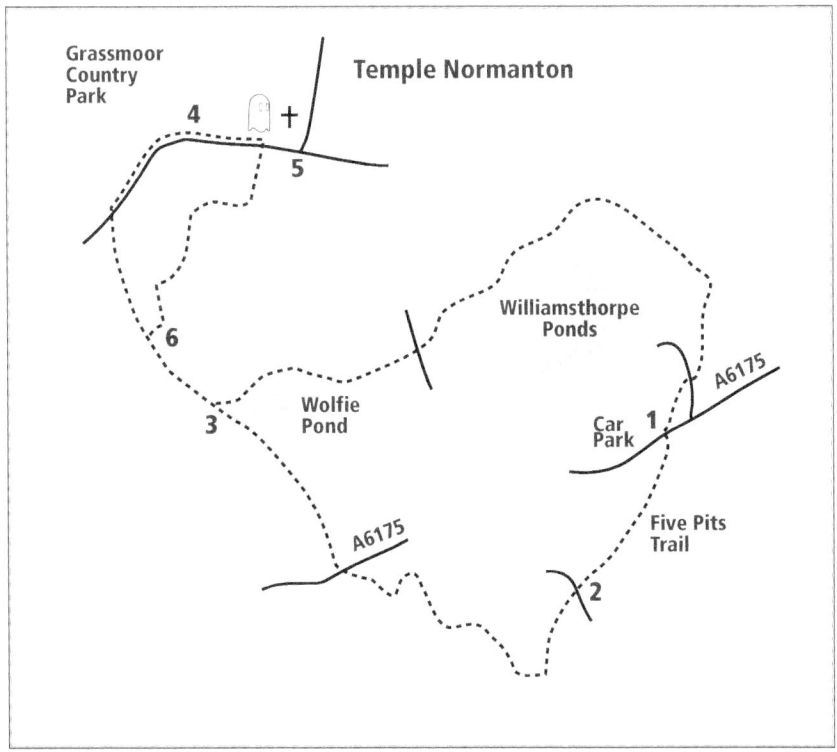

An easy walk on good tracks, mostly on the Five Pits Trail, with only a short section across fields that may be overgrown in midsummer. Open views, an unusual church and ghosts in period costume add to the enjoyment.

On Sundays it is recommended that you try to arrive at Temple Normanton Church at approximately 12 o'clock to be able to see inside it after the service. This is 3¼ miles from the start.

Distance: 6¾ miles

Grade: A

Parking: From Junction 29 of the M1, take the A6175. After about 1¼ miles go straight over a roundabout. Then after 500 yards turn left at the blue 'P' parking sign at the Holmewood Medical Centre.

Map Ref: SK 434658. Explorer 269 Chesterfield Map.

Pub Stop: None.

Route

1. Leave on a path at the bottom of the car park, opposite the entrance, to reach the Five Pits Trail. Turn right then right again at the corner. Stay on the trail until you reach a road.

2. Turn left and immediately right, crossing the road back on to the Five Pits Trail. Where the path divides, go right. At the next junction go right, following the Five Pits Trail to Grassmoor. Stay on the trail until you reach a road (A6175). Cross straight over and back on to the Five Pits Trail.

3. After about ½ mile, you reach Wolfie Pond, which is a pleasant place for a coffee stop. At a junction of paths, where one joins from the right, go left then bear right after 20 yards at the next junction, still following the Five Pits Trail to Grassmoor. Continue on the trail until you reach a bridge over it and a sign for 'Grassmoor Country Park'. Bear right and continue ahead. When, after approximately 300 yards, you reach a car park, turn right into it and right on to the road.

4. Turn left and ascend the hill, taking care when the pavement ends. As you near the top of the hill, note a footpath in the hedge to your right as this is your route. First, continue for a few more yards to Church Lane, Temple Normanton, and turn left.

In 1982 at 7pm, on a summer night in full daylight, Christine Carlisle was driving up the road that you have just walked, approaching Temple Normanton. She was driving very slowly because of the hill, and she glanced to the left just before Church Lane. She was very surprised to see two figures

in period costume two or three yards from her, standing in what appeared to be the entrance of a drive. The lady was wearing a crinoline dress, with her fair hair taken up on top and hanging down at the back. The man had a handlebar moustache. They were completely still, and Christine even wondered if they were mannequins from a shop.

She passed them, but when she glanced in her rear view mirror, they had disappeared. She turned around to look but there was no sign of them. The following week, when she came this way, she decided to investigate and stopped at the same spot. Looking through the trees where she had seen the couple, she realised that it wasn't the entrance to a house as she had assumed. Behind the trees was the graveyard!

Continue down the lane past the cemetery to reach the Parish Church of St James the Apostle. This unusual structure is the fourth church to be built on this site, the former ones having collapsed due to subsidence, having been built over old mine workings. Its design was chosen for its lightness, ability to withstand wind and cheapness according to the vicar!

There is a service held on a Sunday morning at 11.30am, and it is worth

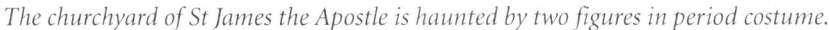

The churchyard of St James the Apostle is haunted by two figures in period costume.

arriving at approximately 12 o'clock in order to see inside this charming place of worship with its lovely interior.

There was never a temple at Temple Normanton. The 'Normanton' says that it was 'the farm of the Norwegians' and temple tells us that it was an estate or hospice belonging to the Knights Templar.

5. Return to the road, turning right and then left at the footpath. Go over the stile and straight ahead in the field, to walk with the hedge on your left. At the end of the field, go over another stile, keeping straight ahead over a small wooden bridge. Bear slightly right up the hill, continuing round to the right, with the hedge on your left-hand side, to finally reach a stile in the left-hand corner. Bear left across the next field, keeping the pylon on your left to reach two stiles in the hedge. Go over them and turn left up the field, with the hedge on your left, to a stile 20 yards from the top left corner. Go over the stile and ahead with hedge on your left. Proceed on to the road and straight ahead. Continue past the buildings to the boundary of the property. Go left on the tarmac area, heading for a wooden arch in the garden. Just before it, turn right on a cinder path, taking you adjacent to the hedge on the right to a stile hidden in the corner. Go up the field with the hedge on your right, looking out for a stile in the hedge after about 50 yards. Go over it and straight across the field, and then through a gateway to reach a track.

6. Turn left. When you reach another track, turn left and take the left fork past the other side of Wolfie Pond. Stay on the trail, ignoring the fork to the left just before a bridge over the trail. Keep right past the sign for 'Williamsthorpe Ponds'. Stay on the track, eventually dropping down the hill, across the bridge, crossing a track and up the other side. Continue straight ahead until you reach a T junction.

Turn left then turn right on the road, following sign for 'Five Pits Trail, Holmewood, over Bridge'. Cross the bridge, then on the far side turn left on the Five Pits Trail. When you reach the road, cross straight over and follow the sign for 'Holmewood Woodland'. After 500 yards, when you reach a crossing of paths and signs for the Five Pits Trails for Tibshelf and for Williamsthorpe, turn right back into the car park.

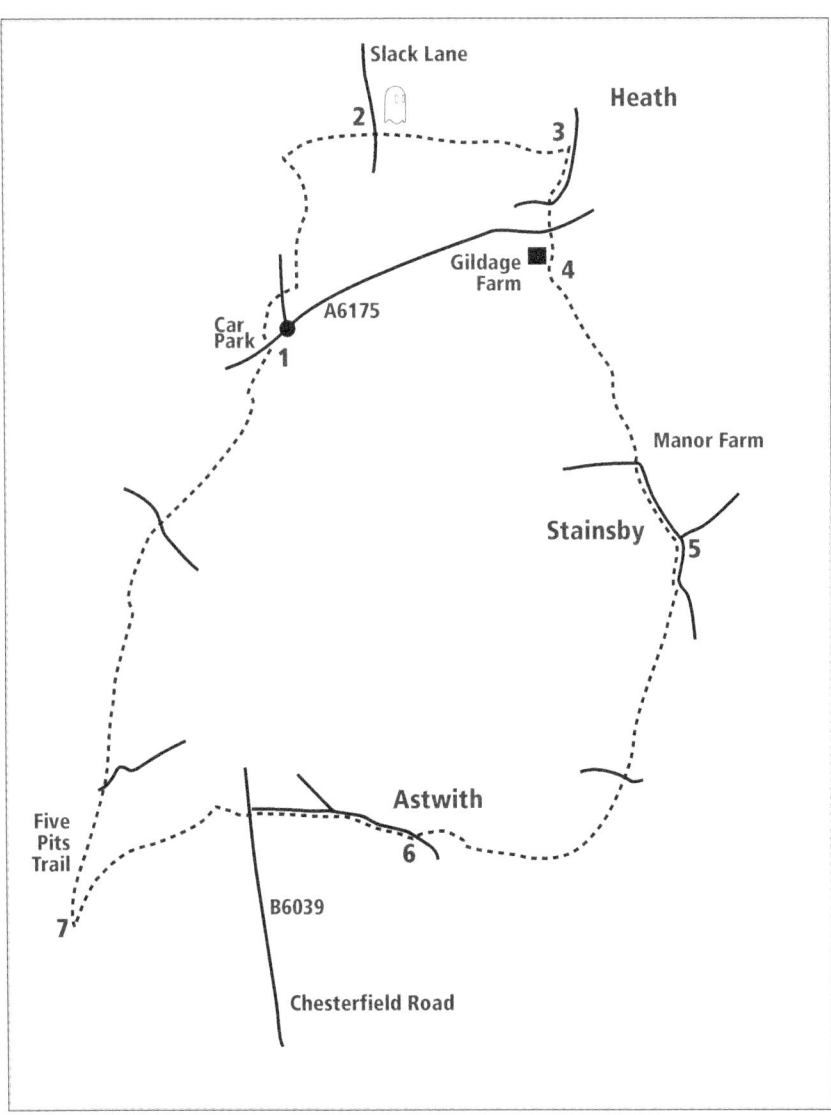

This is a pleasant walk across fields and on lanes, roads and tracks. It has open views of the north Derbyshire countryside and may be enlivened by an encounter with a ghostly, bespectacled nun!

Distance: 6¼ miles
Grade: A
Parking: From Junction 29 of the M1, take the A6175. After about 1¼ miles, go straight over a roundabout. Then after 500 yards turn left at blue 'P' parking sign on the right at the Holmewood Medical Centre.
Map Ref: SK 434658. Explorer 269 Chesterfield Map.
Pub Stop: None.

Route

1. From the car park, go through iron barriers at the bottom end of the car park (the opposite end to the entrance) on to a paved track and turn left, signposted to 'Williamsthorpe'. Keep straight ahead, ignoring the left fork, to reach the road. Cross over and back on to the Five Pits Trail, continuing until you reach another road. Turn right and cross the bridge over a road, then after 30 yards turn left at the Five Pits Trail. Where the path divides, turn right. Pass a sign for 'Williamsthorpe Ponds', then at a footpath sign for 'Heath Village ¾m' turn right.

2. Keep straight ahead on this path until you reach the road.

This is Slack Lane and was where Graham Burton was walking one winter's night on his way home from the Elm Tree Inn when he saw a nun approaching. He remembers that he felt cold and uneasy. As she drew closer, he noticed she was wearing spectacles and seemed to float past. He turned to look after her and received a dreadful shock when she slowly disappeared. He dashed home, arriving white and shaking.

Some years later, after moving house, he and his wife met a Mrs James, a former neighbour from Slack Lane, at a New Year's Eve party. She asked if he could remember his encounter with the vanishing nun and told him that her husband Anthony had also seen the ghost in nun's attire several years after his incident, and that she too was wearing spectacles.

Apparently there was a convent at one time on Shire Lane, off Slack Lane, but why the ghost should be wearing spectacles remains a mystery.

Cross the road and on to the public footpath opposite. Continue forward, adjacent to the hedge on the right, for three fields. At the end of the third, turn left, then after 20 yards turn right over a stile, going ahead to reach the road.

3. Turn right. Where the road turns sharp right, go straight ahead, passing Corner Farm Cottage on your left, to reach the main A6175 road. Turn left then almost immediately right on to a tarmac lane and go over the stile by the iron gate. Go straight ahead, with the farm to the right, on a stony lane.

4. When you reach an iron gate on the left, go over a stile at the side of it and down the field, with the fence on your right and the main road straight ahead in the distance. Go over the stile into the following field, continuing in the same direction, now with hedge on your left. Cross the bridge over the stream at the bottom, up the rise and over the stile. Bear left in the field, towards the house. Go over the next stile and bear left, keeping the house to your right, to reach a stile leading on to a lane by the Stainsby Centre. Go straight ahead on the lane, bearing left when you reach a road, and

Slack Lane, where you may see a ghostly bespectacled nun.

continue down the hill to a T junction.

5. Turn right at the T junction, and then where the road bends to the left bear right on to a footpath to walk up two fields, with the hedge on your left, to reach a lane. Cross the lane and go over the stile on the far side. Go ahead in the field with the wood on your right, then after 50 yards bear left on to a footpath going diagonally across the field. Go over the stile and follow the direction of the arrow sign across the following field, marked with yellow-painted sticks.

Go over the stile and bear right, following the direction of the arrow, heading for the houses. At the hedge, turn left to walk with it on your right, then turn right over a stile and cross the bridge over a stream. Continue straight ahead up a field with the fence/hedge on your left. At the top, bear left at the arrow sign and then go over a stile at the top of the stone steps, adjacent to the building on your left. Go ahead on a path through holly bushes and over a stile on to a track.

6. At the junction, turn right on to the road to go past the telephone box on your right. NB there is a comfortable bench here for a lunch break.

Go straight up the road, ignoring the fork to the right, until you reach the main road. Turn left and almost immediately right at the public footpath sign by the stone wall. Go over the stile and continue ahead, then, keeping the buildings to your right, go over two more stiles then diagonally right across a small field to a stile in the corner.

Look out for ostriches in the field to your right.

Go ahead down the following field with the hedge on your left. Follow the path round to the left and right, continuing to the corner of the field. Go ahead on a path, with a wood to your right, to reach a stile leading on to the paved Five Pits Trail.

7. Turn right and continue ahead. When you reach a road, cross over it, go straight through the car park and back on to the trail. Keep straight ahead at a crossing of paths, then where the path divides take the right fork to Holmewood. Ignore the path to the left, continuing to follow signs for

Holmewood. When you reach the road, turn left and then immediately right back on to the trail. Stay on the trail until you reach the iron barriers on the left, leading you into the car park.

Walk 17
FOREMARK RESERVOIR

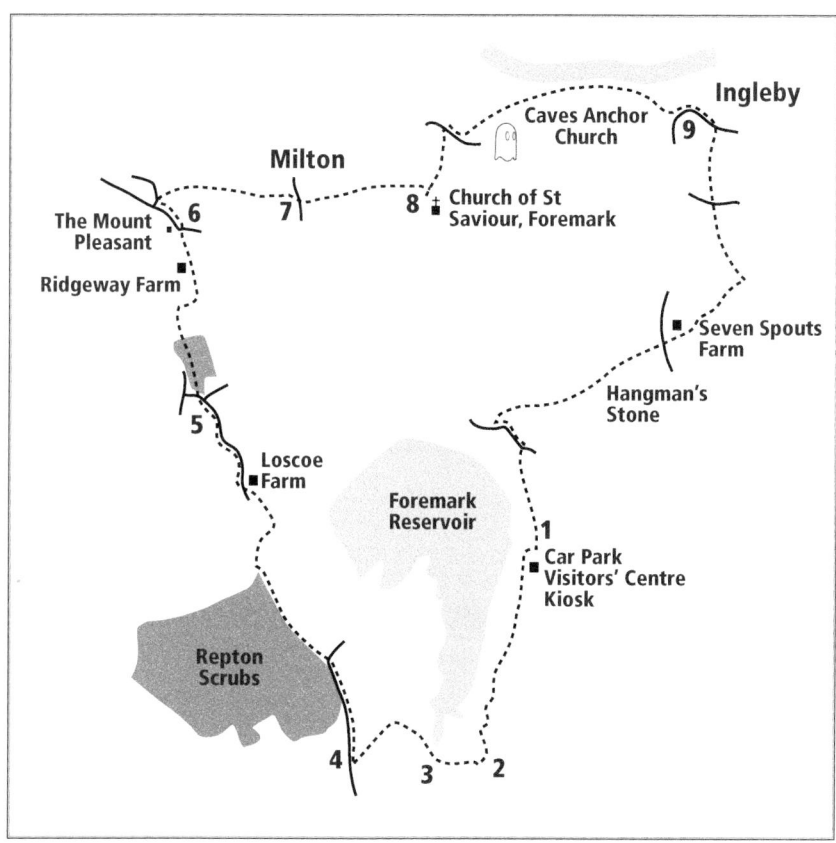

This walk has extensive views throughout, interspersed with a variety of woods, fields and tracks. It visits the unusual Anchor Church and a beautiful stretch of the River Trent.

Note: The section after Anchor Church is on a narrow path, which most walkers will find alright, but any with vertigo may have difficulty because of the drop to the left.

Distance:	10 miles
Grade:	B
Parking:	Foremark Reservoir. Parking charge £1.50 (currently)
Map Ref:	SK 336241. Explorer 245 The National Forest Map.
Pub Stop:	The Mount Pleasant, near Repton, but it is only open 12–2pm Sunday lunch and evenings from 6.30pm. Alternative pub stop: Swan Inn, Milton (See Section 7). Also refreshment kiosk at Foremark Reservoir in car park. Open daily 11am to 4pm (extended at weekends, bank and school holidays). WCs in car park.

The reservoir was built in the 1970s. It holds 2,900 million gallons of water and covers 230 acres.

Route

1. From the car park, pass the kiosk and go towards the reservoir. Cross a gravel path and then turn left on the grassy area nearest to the water. Go ahead on a broad green path, with the reservoir to your right. Upon reaching a footpath to the left for Carver's Rocks, bear left then immediately right, still keeping the reservoir to your right. Pass three paths to the left to Scaddows Oaks. Keep straight ahead until you emerge eventually into a field where there is a signpost.

2. Turn right (this way is not signed). Cross the field, and on the far side bear right through the stile into the nature reserve. Keep straight ahead on this woodland path, passing a nature reserve board and over a wooden bridge. Go over a second wooden bridge and turn right (choice of three paths here) to join a path above the reservoir where you turn left. Keep to the right where some steps come down from the left. Then, where the path divides just after this, turn right following the yellow arrow sign and go over a wooden bridge at the bottom arm of the reservoir.

3. Go up the steps on the far side. Continue straight ahead passing two yellow arrow signs then look for a short flight of steps to the right. Go down them, cross a small wooden bridge and continue ahead until you reach a stile leading you into a field. Bear left up the field, following the direction of the arrow. Go over the stile on the far side, cross the 'gallops' track and through a gate and follow the direction of the arrow up the next field, heading for the right-hand end of the wood. Go through another gate and on to a path with the wood to your left. At the end of the path, go through a kissing gate and straight ahead adjacent to the hedge on your left. Go through a second kissing gate on to the road.

4. Turn right. Keep straight ahead. After ½ mile, where the tarmac road bends right, go on to a track bearing left at an iron gate. Go down the cart track with the wood on your left. Continue on it for about a mile to reach an iron gate. Go through a gap at the side on to a road (at Loscoe Farm). Go straight ahead on the road for nearly ½ mile to a T junction.

5. Cross over the road and on to the footpath opposite, through a gap at the side of an iron gate. Go through the woodland, keeping left on the lower path where it forks, to eventually leave the trees and reach a stile. Go over it into a field with a stream to your left. Continue ahead in the field. When you reach a bridge on your left, turn right and go up the field. Go over the stile in the hedge at the top and across the following field, with the hedge on your right. Climb over a second stile and turn left in the field. Go through an open gateway and continue with the hedge on your left. Keep straight ahead when you reach the farm buildings (Ridgeway Farm) and ahead on a cart track to reach the road and the pub, the Mount Pleasant.

6. Go left on the road and continue ahead until, just past the 30 limit sign, you reach Springfield Road on your right. Turn right, then after 50 yards turn right again at the public footpath sign. Go between the fences then ahead in a field, the path bearing right on the far side to a stile in the hedge. Continue straight across the next two fields. In the fourth field go ahead with the hedge on your right. Go into a green lane, over a stile at the end and on to a tarmac area. Go under the bridge and bear right to the main road.

7. Turn right and almost immediately left, just past a house on the opposite side, at a public footpath sign, which is hidden on a tree (before a telephone box).

For a pub stop, continue past the telephone box for 250 yards. The Swan Inn is on the left. The proprietor will cater for groups by prior arrangement.
(Tel 01283 703188)

Go down between a fence and a wall and over the stile at the end. Continue down two fields with the wall/hedge on your left. Cross the stile at the bottom and over a bridge then another stile and ahead on a broad grassy path. Go through an iron gate and straight ahead across two fields to reach a cart track. Turn right here to visit the church, which is most attractive.

The Church of St Saviour Foremark was consecrated in 1662. The font is believed to date from the 13th century, but the wooden cover was supplied at the time the church was built. It has original box pews and a

Anchor Church is haunted by a hermit, a monk and a young lady in white.

triple-decked pulpit. The lesson for the day is read from the lowest desk, the service conducted from the next and the sermon preached from the top. The church was restored between 1954 and 1964 at a cost of over £8,000. This included scraping the paint from the wonderful oak beams of the roof to restore their natural colouring.

8. On leaving the church, turn right, returning to the cart track. Continue down the lane to reach the road. Turn right (not over the public footpath ahead). Ignore an unmarked stile by a gate after 20 yards. Stay on the road for another 100 yards then go over a stile on the left at a public footpath sign. Bear slightly right across the field, following the footpath arrows to come on to a track. Turn right and cross a stile by an iron gate. Keep straight ahead at a crossing of paths. Go over a stile and ahead on a path beneath the rocks and past a cave, continuing with water to your left (a backwater of the River Trent) until you reach the large caves of Anchor Church.

The Legend of the Severed Hand
In the 12th century Sir Hugo de Burdett and his wife Johanne were very happily married and living in nearby Knowle Hill. However, the Baron of Boyvill, a distant relative of Hugo's, desired Johanne for himself and bribed Bernard, a travelling friar, to persuade Hugo to go to the Crusades. While he was away, Johanne spent her time embroidering a beautiful altar cloth with gold and silver thread and her own hair.

One day Bernard arrived with the news that Sir Hugo had been captured and was being held to ransom. Johanne gave him enough gold to secure his release, but months went by without word. Then, about a year later, the baron came to tell her that Sir Hugo was dead, and that he intended to make her his wife with or without her consent.

Because Boyvill wouldn't give the friar any more money, Bernard secured the release of Sir Hugo and sent word to him that his wife and the baron were both false.

On his return, Sir Hugo met the baron in the woods of Foremark and killed him. He went to his home, still believing that Johanne had been unfaithful, and when she rushed to meet him, overjoyed that he was alive, he drew his sword and severed her left hand, on which she wore her wedding ring, and she bled to death.

Bernard, the friar, was overcome with remorse and became a hermit at Anchor Church, punishing himself in penance so that his cries were heard from afar. Finally, on his death bed, he sent for Sir Hugo and revealed the whole terrible tale. Sir Hugo built a monastery at Ancote in Warwickshire in expiation of his crime, and the altar cloth that Johanne had embroidered was taken there. It is said that anyone who prayed there who had problems with their hands were miraculously cured.

The hermit's ghost haunts Anchor Church, together with a wandering monk and a young lady in white who glides along the riverbank. Young virgins were often sacrificed in days gone by to appease the river gods, and it would seem that her spirit remains tied to the place for which she gave her life.

About 50 yards after Anchor Church, where the rock face ends, turn right where the path forks, leaving the river path, which can become very muddy and submerged. After another 50 yards, turn left at another fork, up a steep bank, keeping the water to your left. Take care on a narrow path with a steep drop to your left, which brings you to the River Trent. When you reach a stile, go over it and bear diagonally right for 20 yards, then left on to a path through the gorse bushes, again parallel to the river on your left. Just before some houses, go over a stile and ahead between the fences.

You may see llamas in the fields to your left!

Go through a wooden gate, over another stile and continue ahead down the field to an iron gate on to a road.

9. Turn left and go round the bend in the road, then turn right at the public footpath sign and up a stony track. Go past the house and continue ahead beside a stone wall on to a woodland track. When you emerge from the woodland, go through a wooden gate and bear left, following the blue arrow sign. At the second arrow, cross the next field with the hedge on your left. Go through the iron gate on the far side and straight over the lane on to the public footpath opposite. Go ahead with the hedge on your right. When the track ends, go straight across the next field. On the far side go into the woodland and turn right on a broad soil track. Ignore the path to the left by the pond. You will eventually reach some buildings, which is 'Seven Spouts Farm.'

This was named after the seven springs or spouts which bubble out of nearby rock formations. At one time these were the only source of water for the whole of Ingleby. Even now there are a few houses which rely solely on this spring water.

10. Go left on the tarmac lane (ignoring the cart track sharp left) with the house to your right. Where the tarmac lane bends to the right, leave it and go straight ahead to reach a road. Cross it and go through the gate at the public bridleway sign. Go ahead across three fields with the hedge on your left. About 50 yards before the end of the third field, note the stone to your left.

This stone, with its peculiar indentation across the top, is associated with a legend that is attached to various stones like this through England. This one is known as the Little Hangman's Stone. At one time there was also a Greater Hangman's Stone, which was five or 6ft high. The story suggests that a thief, having stolen a sheep, tied it by a rope to his neck. He rested by the stone, placing his ill-gotten gains on the top of it. Unfortunately, it slipped off and strangled him, the indentation across the top of the stone being caused by the friction of the rope as the man struggled to release himself.

Going into the fourth field, ignore the paths to your right and left and keep ahead with the hedge on your left. At the bottom of the field, follow the hedge round to the right. Where the trees end and an orchard begins, go left into it and turn immediately right, to walk parallel to the field on your right. The path is indistinct but becomes clearer as you progress. Keep straight ahead, ignoring a path to the left, just after the pond. When you reach a track from the right, turn left, continuing down it to the road. Upon reaching the road, turn left then turn right at the sign for 'Foremark Reservoir'. Go up the access road. Pass the road to the right. When you reach a bridleway to the left, bear left on to it. Ignore the first footpath sign to the right at the children's play area. Then, opposite a sign on the left for 'Lamont Wood', turn right through a wooden gate. When you reach a path crossing your own, turn right then left to lead you back into the car park.

Walk 18
CODNOR

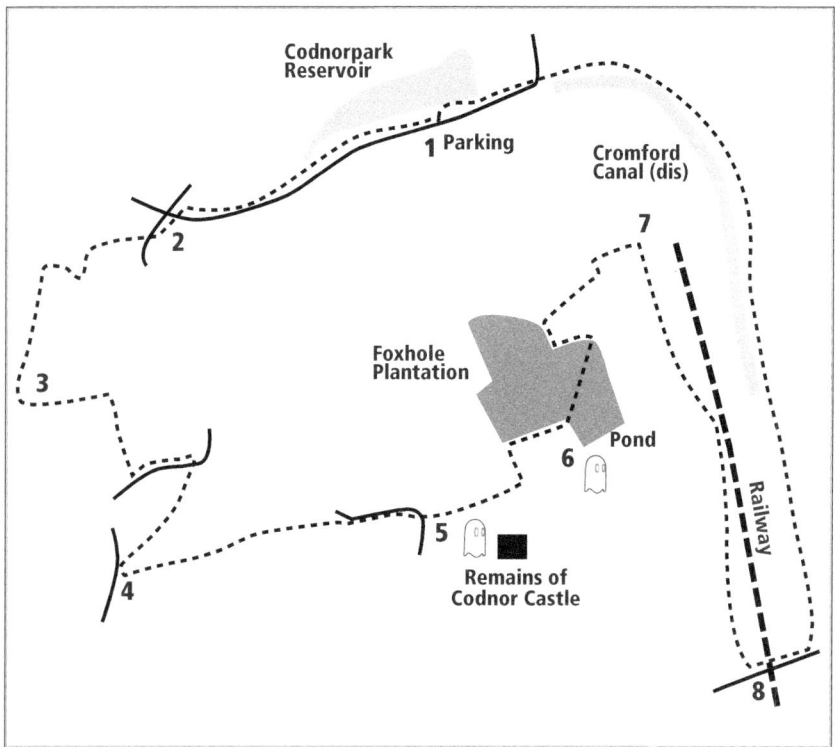

This is an attractive flat walk which starts by the side of Codnorpark Reservoir and goes through fields, woods and along lanes. It returns by way of the old disused Cromford Canal, passing through a nature reserve, and has a variety of wildlife, including the chance of seeing a kingfisher. It can, however, be extremely muddy in parts and is best done after a period of dry weather.

Distance: 7½ miles
Grade: A
Parking: Codnorpark Reservoir.
Map Ref: SK 433515. Explorer 269 Chesterfield Map and very small part
            on Explorer 260 Nottingham Map.
Pub Stop: Stoneyford Lodge (closed all day Monday)

Route

1. From the car park, facing the reservoir, go left along the path. Keep going along this path, then as you leave the reservoir cross an old car park and bear right across the iron bridge. On the far side, go left where the path forks and continue ahead with the canal on your left. Keep left where the path again forks until finally it rises to reach the road opposite the Newlands Inn.

Look out for a kingfisher that has its territory on the latter part of this next section!

2. Turn left. Pass Coach Road to the left and to the right, then after 100 yards turn right through a gap at the side of a wooden gate on to a broad woodland path. Stay on this path as it winds through the wood, emerging eventually by the side of a house, and go over a stile into a field. Go straight ahead in the field, then through a stile at the side of a gate and immediately left at a stile marked 'Amber Valley Walkways No.4'. Go up the field with a hedge on your left. At the far end of the field, go through a stile where you reach a choice of paths.

3. Go left on the path just before the iron railings ahead. Keep straight ahead, then, 100 yards past the end of the works on the right, turn right on to a broad path. Where the path emerges on to a service road, keep ahead down to the main road. Turn left. After 200 yards, turn right at a public footpath sign and go over a stile in the hedge. Follow the direction of the sign to head diagonally across the field. The stile is to the right of the corner near a water trough and by an (open) iron gate. Continuing in the same

Codnor Castle is haunted by a dishevelled Civil War soldier.

direction, go up the next field to a stile in the middle of the hedge, then to a stile by an iron gate in the next field. In the following field, go straight ahead, with the hedge on your left, to a stile by the white house, leading on to a track.

4. Turn left. Go over a stile and ahead in the field with a hedge on your left. At the end of the field, go straight ahead up the hill and continue ahead on a well-defined path to emerge eventually on to a paved road. Turn right. Follow the road round to the right, then 20 yards after the right-hand bend turn left over a stile in the hedge.

5. Follow the direction of the arrow sign across the field.

To your right are the ruins of the 13th-century Codnor Castle, a stone keep and bailey fortress established by William Peveril. In 1211 it was owned by Henry de Grey, whose descendants included Lady Jane Grey. It was a place of considerable size with a large, square court on its south side and a broad deep moat to the east, and it stood in a park of about 2,200 acres. However, it has not been occupied since the 18th century.

The ghost of a stray soldier from Cromwell's army has been seen in the ruins, appearing dishevelled, unshaven and worn out, although the castle and its inhabitants do not seem to have any specific connection to the English Civil War.

Continue across the field to the left-hand corner, then go down the next field to the bottom left-hand corner. Go through a kissing gate and turn left. (An alternative footpath to that shown on the Ordnance Survey map has been provided at this point. The right of way is diagonally right and will be reinstated at some point, taking you directly to the corner of the wood at the pond.) Walk ahead along the footpath between the fences and pass through a kissing gate immediately before a wood. Turn right and follow the path along the edge of a wood to the bottom corner of a field. When you reach the bottom corner, climb the stile into Foxhole Plantation and pause at the pond.

On a sunny spring morning a young motorcyclist stopped at this pond for a cigarette. Leaning against a tree, he saw two young girls emerge from an area by the pond. They stared at him then took a path leading away from him. The eldest, who led the way, had blonde hair and was about seven or eight years old. The younger one looked about six and had brown hair.

Although they had come from the muddiest part of the pond, there was not a speck of dirt on them. They were dressed in what he thought was 1940s clothing. He followed them and called to ask if they were alright, but they didn't reply.

At the edge of the wood, they climbed the stile and headed towards Kennels Farm. By this time the youth was caked in mud, but the children remained spotless. As he moved to follow them across the field, the youngest turned round and said 'You can't come'. They continued over the field and then, without warning, vanished.

6. Aligning your back to the stile, your path through the wood lies at 1 o'clock across the pond. It may be helpful to send a member of your party around the pond to act as a marker. Contour around the end of the pond and take a path going up through the wood. At the top right-hand corner, go over a stile into the field. (An alternative footpath to that shown on the Ordnance Survey map is also provided at this point. Right of way was straight ahead and will be reinstated at some point.) Turn left. With the wood now on your left, go ahead to the corner and follow it round to the right. At the end of the field, go through a gap in the hedge and turn right. Go down two fields with the hedge on your right. Go through a kissing gate then over a stile and ahead between the fences to reach a track. (When the footpaths are reinstated, you will go straight ahead from leaving Foxhole Plantation and will come to this track a little further along to the right and can, therefore, continue the route.)

7. Turn right. After 300 yards go over the stile by a gate, (by Kennels Farm) and keep ahead. Go over a second stile by a gate. Ignore the path to the right and keep straight ahead through the woodland. Pass a footbridge over the railway to the left (don't go over it) and continue in the same direction until you leave the wood and go ahead on a path between the fences. After passing under electricity wires, the path goes right and left to emerge over a stile into a field. Go straight across two fields to a stile in the hedge, midway between the houses, to reach a lane and your pub stop at Stoneyford Lodge.

8. Turn left on the lane, over a railway bridge and down a hill. Just past the house, go through the stile on the right by the side of the gate, then turn left at the public footpath sign. Go over a stile and on to the Cromford Canal footpath. Keep straight ahead. After ¾ mile you will reach a stile at the brickwork of the old disused railway. Go over it, cross the bridge and then continue in the same direction as before. After another ½ mile, when you reach a stone bridge on your left, go over it and take the left path where it forks, bringing you back to the canal. Continue on this path with the canal to your left for another mile until you reach the Codnorpark Reservoir. Go left over the footbridge and back into the car park.

WALK 19
TICKNALL

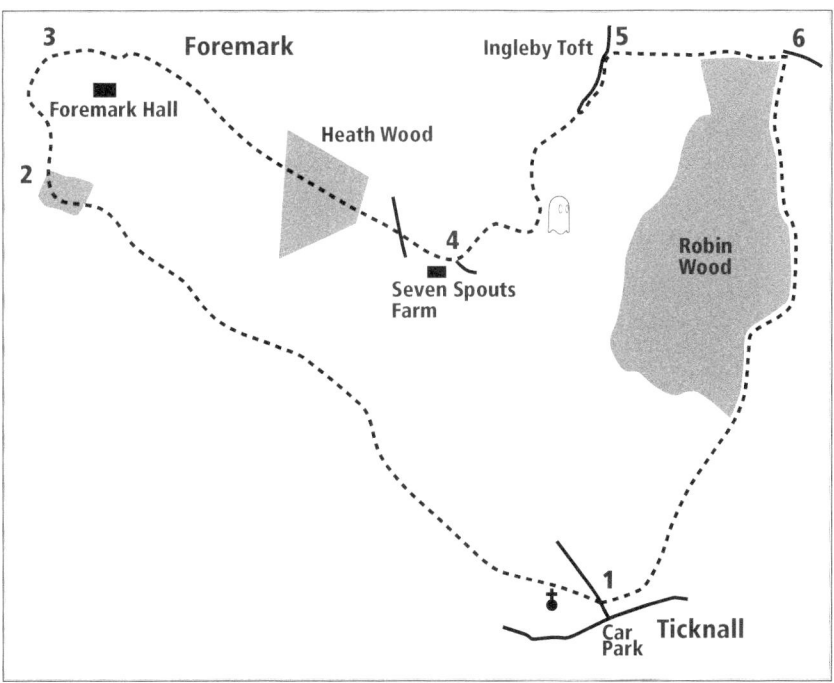

This is a gentle walk from Ticknall, covering an area of rolling countryside to the west of Melbourne. It is mainly on good tracks, although these may be muddy after long periods of rain, and holds a wealth of interest.

Distance: 7 miles
Grade: A
Parking: Village Hall car park, Ticknall. Look for the 'P' sign for parking and WCs on the main A514 road through Ticknall opposite the Wheel Inn. WCs in the car park.
Map Ref: SK 353241. Explorer 245 the National Forest Map.

Pub Stop: None.

The Church of St George, which you can see, was built in 1831 on the site of the Church of Thomas Beckett. This former church proved so difficult to demolish, even when gunpowder was used, that parts of it, namely the west wall and the altar window, remain standing.

Route

1. From the car park, go towards the church and then over a stile in the fence on the right. Follow the direction of the arrow in the field, keeping the church to the left. Go over another stile and ahead with the wall/hedge to the left. Pass a footpath on the left, and when you come to a track go straight over and continue across the next field, with the hedge on your left. Go through a gate and cross the following field. Continue in the same direction on a broad track between a hedge and a fence. Go through another gate and continue with the hedge on your left. At the next gate, continue forward, then at a further gate, proceed in the same direction but now with the hedge on the right-hand side. Join a track coming in from the right and continue ahead. Where the track goes to the left, leave it to go under the power lines, now keeping the hedge on the left-hand side. Go through the wood.

2. At the end of the wood, turn right across the field, heading for the buildings. When you reach Home Farm, go straight through on to the lane to reach a church, which is well worth a visit. (See Walk 17 for information.) Continue down the lane and turn right on to a track at a sign for Foremark Hall HGV entrance.

3. Go past the hall on your right.

Foremark Hall was built in 1755 by Sir Robert Burdett on the site of a very ancient house of the Francis family. It is now the Preparatory Department of Repton School and houses approximately 390 boys and girls from the ages of three to 13, 120 of whom board overnight.

Follow the road between the buildings. Where the road goes left at a postbox, leave it to go straight ahead on a track, passing Ash Cottage on your right. Continue on this broad track between the trees. When you reach a sign for 'Heath Wood', go over the stile and through the wood. Leave the wood by a stile near a gate and continue in the same direction, going through a double line of trees until you reach a road. Cross over the road, bearing right, and go down the track opposite. When you reach the buildings (Seven Spouts Farm), take the left hand of three tracks.

4. When you reach a small lake, turn right at the end of it and up the path. Go over the stile at the top and then left through the gate, taking care to close it after you. Go straight across the field.

The building to your right is Knowle Hill House. It is said that an underground tunnel once linked Knowle Hill with Anchor Church,

Knowle Hill is haunted by a dejected knight.

which you visit in Walk 17, and its ghostly tale is similarly linked. On moonlit nights at Knowle Hills the figure of a knight in armour has been seen walking around this green. When he reaches where Johanne's bedchamber would have been, he utters a dejected sigh and then disappears.

On the far side of the field, go left over a stile and down through the wood. When you reach the track, turn right. Continue ahead, with the wood on your right, until you reach a road.

Your route here lies straight ahead, but it is worth taking a short diversion up the lane to your left to see the imposing entrance and house of 'Ingleby Toft'. This is a Queen Anne style house, built *c.*1732 as a dower house by the Burdetts of Foremark.

I'm not sure I would want to glimpse the lions on a murky night. They look a little too real!

Go straight ahead on the lane, then when you reach a drive on the left for Ingleby Toft turn right on the public bridleway opposite.

5. Go down the field and ahead, up through the wood. Continue ahead, leaving the wood and then passing through an iron gate on to a paved lane. Go past Wood End Cottage, then turn right at the second iron gate immediately past the cottage.

6. Go into a field and follow its boundary on the right. Continue with the woodland on your right for about ¾ mile. When you reach the radio mast, keep by the edge of the wood then pass by the sub station. Cross the track beyond, and go ahead with the fence of Vee Wood on your left (planted in 2000) and Robin Wood to the right.

Robin Wood is associated with Sir Francis Burdett, the fifth Baronet of Foremark, who was born in 1770. Described as a noble and courageous man, he was renowned for his radical views on the laws of the land and for being a champion of the people. Our right of free speech today is due

largely to his denouncement of the injustice of the government preventing freedom of discussion. At one time, he was imprisoned in the Tower of London and fined the enormous sum of £40,000. To pay for this, all the oak trees in Robin Wood had to be felled and sold as timber.

When you come to the end of the wood, go left, walking between fences then ahead across a field. On the far side, cross a lane and continue ahead to walk between a fence and hedge. Where the path is divided by a hedge, keep to the right, to walk with the fence on your right. At the end of the fence, go straight ahead over a stile in the hedge into the field beyond. Follow the direction of the arrow across the field. In the next field, bear right towards the buildings to reach a small gate at a public bridleway sign. Go through the gate and turn right on to a narrow lane between the houses. Continue until you reach the road. Turn right and then left back into the car park.

Ticknall has some interesting buildings and is worth a walk around. There are 14 lion's head waterpipes within it, provided by the Harpur Crewe family in 1914.

WALK 20
SHARDLOW

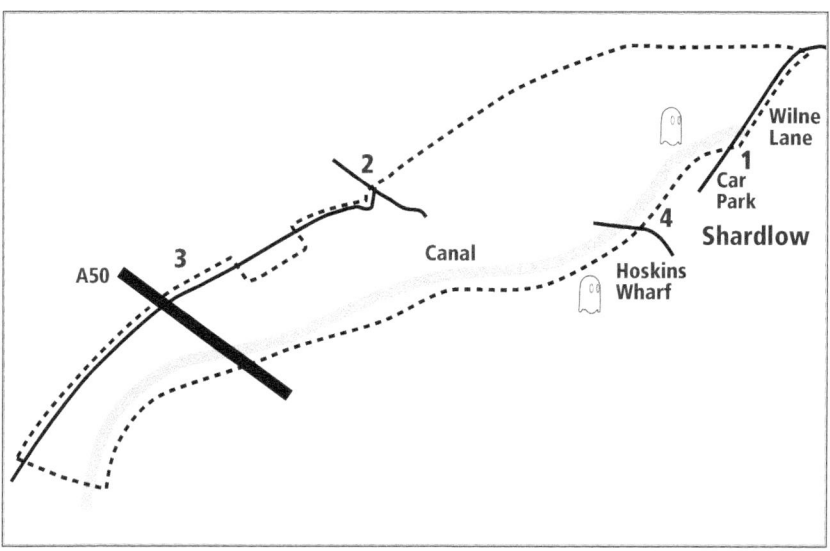

This is an easy flat walk by the canal side, on roads and across fields, with plenty of ghostly interest to enliven each mile.

Distance: 4 miles

Grade: A

Parking: Long stay car park on Wilne Lane, Shardlow. The Navigation Inn marks the end of Wilne Lane in Shardlow.

Map Ref: SK 446305. Explorer 260 Nottingham and Explorer 245. The National Forest Maps.

Pub Stop: Multiple choice! Plus there are the Canal Bank Tea Rooms at Hoskins Wharf, open Saturdays and Sundays at 11am.

Route

1. Leave the car park by the entrance and turn right on the road. Go up the road and cross the humpback bridge over the canal, to where the road turns sharp right. Turn left down a short lane and ahead into the field, to walk with the left of the two hedges on your right. Continue ahead between the hedge and the wall then across three more fields with a hedge on your right. Go through the hedge then ahead on to a cart track and left on top of the flood bank. Bear right to a stile and go over it to walk between a wood to the right and a building to the left. Go straight ahead over two stiles. Follow the direction of the footpath sign in the field then over two more stiles and ahead, to walk between the walls and reach the road.

2. Cross over and go up the road opposite with the Dog and Duck on your right. Follow the road round to the right and left, then 200 yards past the mini roundabout turn left on to Aston Lane. Go along the lane, and after 300 yards turn right across the field. On the far side, go over two stiles and up the steps to the road.

3. Turn left. Cross the bridge over the A50 and continue down the road for ¼ mile, then turn left on to a lane. Go down the lane and cross a bridge over the canal, then turn left along the canal bank. Continue by the canal for about a mile, passing under two bridges and then reaching a lock. Go down the lane, dropping back to the canal bank before the next bridge (Hoskins Wharf).

The building on the right before the bridge is the Old Salt Warehouse, which has a reputation for being haunted. It has been, in its time, a cycle shop, a butcher's, a saddler's and an antiques shop, which Geoff Clifton ran. The old ground floor rooms formed a basement, while customers entered at first-floor level from the road.

There was a corner of one of the basement rooms that was exceptionally cold, which Geoff described as 'like standing in a well of cold water'. His son was extremely sceptical about the phenomenon, but when invited to stand in the spot he agreed that there was a hell of a cold draught. However, when Geoff suggested that he use his cigarette lighter

The Old Salt Warehouse, which has a strange cold spot in its basement

The Malt Shovel, where ghosts may push, nip or poke you.

to test his theory, the flame burned steadily with no sign of any air current to disturb it.

Geoff has no explanation for the strange cold spot, although there are a wealth of ghosts in Shardlow to choose from to attribute it to, including a one-legged pedlar who was murdered in the 18th century.

4. Continue on the canal side.

Note the pub on the far side, the Malt Shovel. It is said that when this was a malt house a worker fell into a boiling vat and died a terrible death. He is said to haunt the cellar. During renovation work, workmen reported being pushed, nipped and poked.

Another inebriated drinker, said to have walked into the canal and drowned, is said to haunt the canal side.

When you reach the next bridge, go up the steps at the side of it to reach the road. Turn right and return down Wilne Lane to the car park on your left.

At the bottom of Wilne Lane on the right is the Lady in Grey restaurant. This is another pub with a ghostly history. This 18th-century property was, until recently, a private house and was owned by the Soresby family. The lady after which the restaurant is named is said to be Jeanette Soresby.

One story says that she was one of two maiden ladies who were devoted to the place. Another says that the ghost is that of a girl who was deprived of her inheritance. The youngest of three daughters, she was promised her mother's jewels. However, her older sisters were jealous of her good fortune, and when their mother died one of them buried the jewels.

The ghost of the young woman is said to hunt for the jewels until this day. Many strange happenings have been reported in the Lady in Grey over the years. Staff and customers have reported the feeling of someone pushing past them and a number have seen the lady in grey in Victorian dress pass through the building.

Harold Kyte's experience when he lived there was nearly fatal. He returned one night to the Lady in Grey from a gig where he had been playing saxophone in a local band. He fancied a steak so went into the walk-in freezer to get one. Although the door was heavy and didn't move easily, it closed behind him trapping him inside.

Luckily his wife came looking for him after about 10 minutes and heard him banging on the inside of the freezer and released him. Both were convinced that the door could not have moved on its own or have been blown shut and are sure that some supernatural hand closed it, imprisoning him. Whether this was the lady in grey herself remains unknown.

The Lady in Grey, where a ghost may push you or lock you in the freezer!

WALK 21
AMBERGATE/WINGFIELD

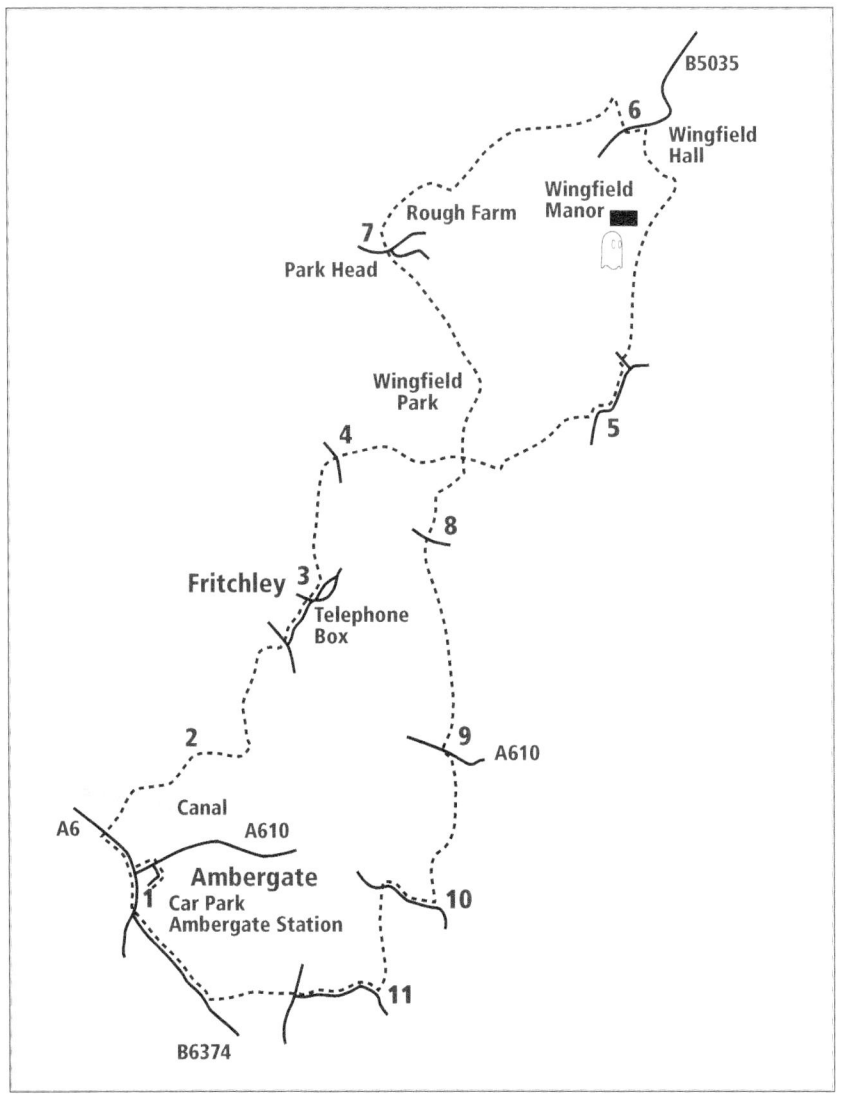

This is an attractive walk in an area to the north east of Ambergate, with open views. It is mostly on good tracks, although these can be muddy after periods of wet weather.

Distance: 8½ miles
Grade: B
Parking: Ambergate Station car park. NB there are WCs to the left of the bridge on the A6 at the A610/A6 junction at the start of the walk.
Map Ref: SK 349516. Explorer 269 Chesterfield Map.
Pub Stop: None.

Route

1. Leave the car park by the access road. Go down to the A610 road and turn left, go under the bridge and turn right, crossing the road. Go 200 yards along the road to Chase Road, where you turn right. Go under the bridge and straight up the road then cross the bridge over the canal. Continue on the road until you reach a wooden gate on the left, with a small gate at the side and a public footpath sign. Go into the field and keep to the right-hand boundary. At the end of the field where it narrows, go through the gap stile and ahead. When you come to a T junction turn left, keeping the works on your right-hand side. Go over a stile into a field and up the hill. Keep to the right-hand boundary, ignoring an arrow sign and path going to the right, and continue uphill until you reach a broad path.
2. Turn right. Continue on this wide path as it climbs steadily uphill. Ignore a stile by a gate and stay on the main path. Where the path narrows between the hedges, continue on it and ahead again where it becomes a broad (muddy) track. Go through a gap stile by a wooden gate and on to a lane. Just after you reach the first house on your right, turn right at a public footpath sign for 'Bullbridge'. Go down the narrow footpath to reach the road. Cross over on to Allen Lane. When you reach a telephone box, keep it to your right and go straight ahead and along Chapel Street.
3. Turn left at the public footpath sign to 'Dimple Lane', going down

Kirkham Lane. Keep straight ahead on the lane. Go through a stile by an iron gate then through the buildings, over a stile and follow the direction of the yellow arrow across the field. Go through a stile on the far side then turn right. Go left through a stile by a gate. Continue ahead, dropping down to a stile leading into woodland then across a bridge over a stream to reach a road.

4. Turn right and almost immediately left at a public footpath sign up a lane, with houses to your left. Stay on the lane, ignoring the footpath to the left at the corner. Follow the sign for 'Wingfield Park'. When you reach two iron gates with the sign 'T S Thorpe, Thorpe Hill', go through the stile on the left and up the track. Where the track bends left, leave it to go straight ahead up the field to join a wall on your right. Go through the stile to the right and into the woodland. Stay on this path as it winds through the woodland, emerging eventually over a stile into a field. Go ahead with a wall on your right. Go through a stile and back into the woodland. On the far side, go ahead on a path between the walls. Continue on this path for about ½ mile, going through stiles and a gate, ignoring paths to the left and right, until you finally reach a road.

5. Go straight ahead and at a T junction turn left, following the sign for Crich and South Wingfield. Just before the first house on the right, turn right through a stile, following an arrow for 'Amber Valley 7'. Go straight up two long fields (the boundaries have been removed) with the hedge on your left. Continue into a third field, now with a wall on your right. At the end, follow the public footpath sign into the next field, now with the wall on your left. Go through a stile by a gate.

The ruins to your left are those of Wingfield Manor, which was built in 1440 by Ralph, Lord Cromwell, Treasurer of England to Henry VI. By the reign of Elizabeth I, the house was owned by the Earl of Shrewsbury and his wife, Bess of Hardwick. They were responsible for the imprisonment of Mary Queen of Scots at Wingfield Manor on the orders of Elizabeth.

Their role as jailors must have been somewhat lax as Mary was allowed visits from Sir Anthony Babbington, who would also steal into

Wingfield Manor is haunted by Mary Queen of Scots and a murdered maid.

the house at night to plot her escape and the downfall of Elizabeth. It is said that he would darken his face with the juice of crushed walnuts so that he could pass as a common man. One walnut is supposed to have fallen from his pocket and grown into the magnificent tree in the courtyard.

Mary's spirit is said to like the ballroom, while spheres of light floating around after dark may or may not be part of the same entity.

Strange blue lights have also been seen flickering in the undercroft and there is another story referred to as the curse of Wingfield Manor, which involves another Mary – a local girl who went to work there in 1666. Mary told another maid, Fanny, of her love for a young farmer, not knowing that Fanny loved the same man.

Fanny lured Mary into the undercroft and locked her in, and her body was not discovered until many years later, when Fanny confessed on her deathbed. Mary's skeleton was found huddled at the top of the stairs behind the locked door and her ghost is said to haunt the area.

The ghostly tales and hauntings are said to be the reason why Wingfield Manor has been left uninhabited since the 1770s.

Continue ahead down the track. When you reach a junction of paths, go left. Go over a stile at the bottom and left on the broad lane. Pass the buildings of Wingfield Hall to your right and continue up the lane to the main road.

6. Cross over and turn left. Go down the hill, past the houses, then look for a yellow arrow sign and public footpath sign for 'Inns Lane' to the right of a wooden gate. Turn right here and ahead across the field, with the hedge to your left. Go over the stile on the far side, and then in the next field go left and over the wooden footbridge. Continue adjacent to the hedge on the left for two fields then straight ahead for two further fields. At the far side of the following (sixth) field, turn right, then after 100 yards turn left through a gap stile in the hedge. Bear right across the field. Go across the next field, first with a wall on your left then, ¾ of the way across, go through a gap stile to walk with the wall on your right. Go past the farm (Rough

Farm) and continue to the top of the field, through a stile to reach a lane. Turn left and go ahead to the main road.

7. Go diagonally across on to Park Lane, signposted Wingfield Park and Pentrich. After 30 yards, just after Old Shaft Farm, turn right at the public bridleway sign. Continue straight down the bridleway, past the farm (Park Farm). Go over a stile by the gate. Stay on the track, then when you come to two gates take the right hand one, following the arrow sign for 'Amber Valley 1'. Where the track ends, continue ahead into the field, with a wall on your left. On the far side, cross the track and go straight ahead through the stile. Continue ahead in the next field parallel to the wall on your left. At the end of the field, go left through the waymarked iron gate. Ignore paths to the right and left and continue straight down the field with the hedge on your right. Go ahead on to a track, to eventually reach a road.

8. Go straight across and down the field with the hedge on your right. Just before the bottom corner, turn right through a stile then left down the next field, now with the hedge on your left. Go through an open gateway and ahead over the next three fields to reach the railway line. Take care crossing the line. Go over the stile on the far side, and in the field head for a bridge on the far side. Cross the bridge and go straight ahead to reach the main A610 road.

9. Cross over and turn left, and after 30 yards go up a steep flight of steps. Bear right over the bridge, across the road and ahead, following the yellow footpath sign. Pass Waterloo Farm and ahead on a path between the walls. Cross a stile into a field, following the sign for 'Amber Valley 5', walking with a wall on your right. At two gateways, go through the right hand one, NOT following the 'Amber Valley 5' sign, and ahead in the field, now with a wall on your left side. Go through the stile to the right of the bottom corner and ahead across the following field, emerging on to a broad lane and continuing to a road.

10. Turn right. Just after two semi-detached houses on the left, at a sign for 'Nether Heage', turn left up a lane by the side of the house called Clovelly. At the top, bear left to a yellow footpath sign then straight ahead across two fields, with the hedge on your right. At the end of the field, go through the gateway, turn left, then after 20 yards turn right over the stile. Go up the field with the hedge on your right. Continue across the following field then through a stile on to a lane then ahead to the road.

11. Turn right and go up the lane. When you reach a T junction, turn left then immediately right through a stile by a gate. Go up the field with a wall on your left. At the top, bear right, cross the lane and go over a stile. Go down the next field with the wall on your right. At the bottom right-hand corner, go ahead on a narrow path between a wall and fence. Continue until you reach a road. Turn right down the hill. When you reach the main road (A6) turn right then right again at the junction. Go under the bridge and then right up the access road back to the car park.

WALK 22
WESTON UNDERWOOD

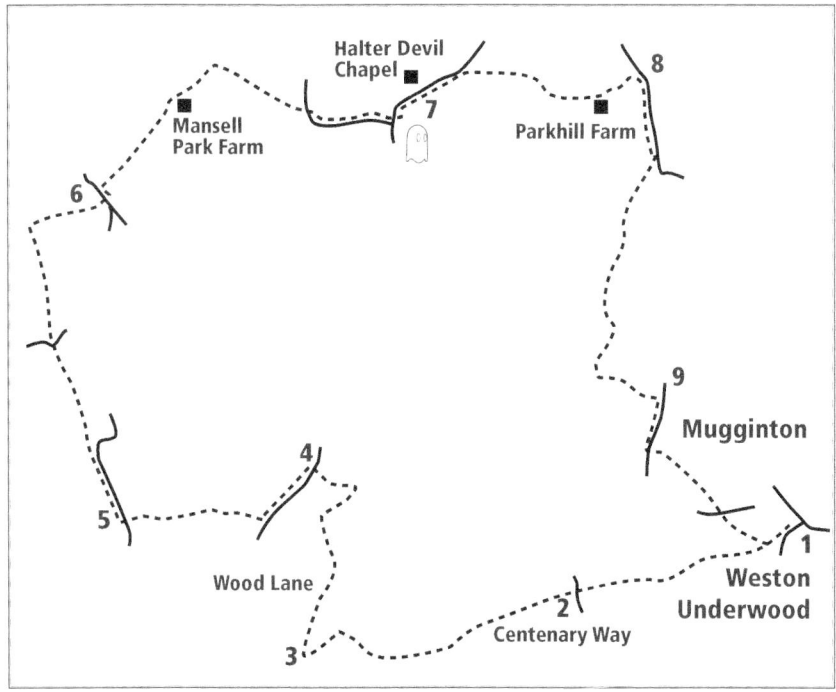

This is an undulating walk to the north west of Derby. It has good views and a visit to the strangely named Halter Devil Chapel adds additional interest.

It is, however, best avoided in late summer as stiles become overgrown at this time and crops obscure footpaths in fields with no distinct path left by farmers.

Distance: 9½ miles
Grade: B
Parking: Limited parking is available on Cutler Lane in Weston

Underwood, which is the first road on the left off the main road when approaching from the Derby/Kedleston direction. This is also the starting point of the walk.

Map Ref: SK 292424. Explorer 259 Derby Map.

Pub Stop: None.

Route

1. Go up Cutler Lane, then after 50 yards, just after the farmyard entrance, turn right up a short flight of steps and over a stile on the Centenary Way. Follow the direction of the footpath sign, bearing slightly left to the bottom left-hand corner of the field. Go over a stile and bridge and straight ahead up the field, continuing to follow the Centenary Way. Cross the next field and bear left in the following one. Cross a bridge over a stream (Mercaston Brook) and proceed up the next field with the fence on your left. Go through a kissing gate on to the lane and continue straight ahead up the track. At the top of the lane, go over two stiles and ahead in the field. On the far side, go over a stile into a lane.

2. Cross over, bearing right over a stile into a field, and follow the direction of the footpath sign up the field. Follow the contour of the field where it bends right and left, to continue adjacent to the right-hand boundary. At the top right-hand corner, follow the direction of the arrow sign into the field beyond. Where the boundary hedge goes right, leave it and go straight ahead. On the far side, go over a wooden bridge and through a gate in the left-hand corner. Go across the next short field and over a stile and follow the arrow, bearing right in the following one. Go over a stile near the top-right corner and follow the arrow sign ahead in the next field. Go under the power lines and over a wooden bridge into the last field and go left, to walk adjacent to the hedge on your left side, emerging on to a track (Wood Lane) on the far side.

3. Turn right. Stay on the lane for about ½ mile but look for a post with a yellow arrow sign on the left hand side at the second gate. (This is about 200 yards after where the power lines come close on the left and then move away. If you reach a road you have come too far.) Head across the field to a gap stile in the hedge at a point midway between the house and the electricity pylon. Go round the building on your right, through the gap at the back of it, then left to a gate on to a road.

4. Turn left and cross over. When you reach the buildings on the left, go through a gate opposite them and straight across a field. Ignore the arrow signs to the right and left. Cross the next field to a stile in the hedge, midway between the two cottages. Follow the direction of the arrow, bearing left up the field, passing a pond to your right, then head for the top right-hand corner of the field, keeping a small copse of trees on your right, to reach a road.

5. Turn right. Go past a road to the right, then 50 yards after the Z-bend sign turn left on a track to North Farm. After 50 yards, where there is a metal gate on the right, turn right to find a stile hidden in the hedge into the woodland. Pass through the trees into the field beyond and straight ahead with a hedge on your left-hand side, heading for the white house. Cross the track and continue ahead in a field, still with the hedge on your left. Continue in the same direction in the next field then cross a lane. Go ahead between the wood on your left and fence on your right for about 50 yards, then pass through the hedge on the left and turn right, to walk now with the hedge on your right for two fields. At the end of the second field, bear left to cross the dyke to a stile about 50 yards along the hedge.

Follow the arrow sign and go straight ahead up the following field. As you approach the far side, look for a lone tree and head for it. The stile is hidden in the hedge beyond it, at the right-hand end of the holly hedge.

Turn immediately right and go up the field with the hedge on your right, continuing in the following field to reach the road.

6. Turn left past the buildings and then right at the footpath sign into the field, then continue along a track to Mansell Park Farm, with the fence on your right. Go past the farm, through an iron gateway, then diagonally right across the following field, to the right-hand corner by the buildings. Go through the wooden gate and turn right on the paved track, continuing until you reach the road. Turn right, and then at the T junction turn left on Intakes Lane. After 300 yards, look for the sign for the 'Halter Devil Chapel' on your left and go up the drive to have a look at this tiny chapel with its strange story.

A key may be obtained from the farm if you wish to view the interior. A small contribution to the chapel's restoration and upkeep would, I'm sure, be appreciated.

The chapel was built by Francis Brown in 1723. There are various versions of the story of how he came to build it. He was a hard-drinking man and was also said to have misappropriated some public funds.

One stormy night, he decided he would ride to Derby and went out to the field to saddle his horse. But the horse was chasing about, frightened by the storm, and he couldn't catch it. In drunken anger Francis Brown

The Halter Devil Chapel built after the Devil reformed a drinker!

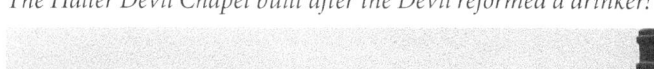

cried 'If I can't halter thee, I'll halter the Devil!' Whereupon there was a flash of lightning and he was confronted with a black-horned face.

Now, some may say that, as he was the worse for drink, he had tried to halter a cow instead of his horse, but he was terrified by what had happened. He became a reformed man, built the chapel and endowed it with land.

7. Return to the road and turn left to continue in the same direction as before for another 300 yards. Turn right at a footpath on the right. Follow the direction of the footpath sign to pick up a yellow arrow sign and continue to the bottom of the field, to pass between the two ponds. Cross a footbridge then follow the yellow arrow sign up the field. Go over a stile at the gateway at the top of the field then ahead to a stile by an iron gate. Bear right on a broad grassy track, contouring round the hill. Continue through Parkhill Farm, staying on the track until it eventually reaches a main road.

8. Turn right. Pass a post box and the Park Farm entrance. Ignore a stile with a public footpath sign in the hedge, then 200 yards beyond this turn right opposite a footpath sign situated on the left-hand side of the road. Go down the track. When you reach the buildings, go over the stile to the left then immediately right past the horse trough. Go down the field with the hedge on your right. At the bottom of the field, turn right over the fencing. Pass through a shrubby area, bearing left to a gap stile. Go ahead in the field, through a wooden gate to the left then turn right to walk with the hedge/fence on your right. At the end of the wood, go through a wooden gate then bear left and right towards the buildings. Go through the iron gate at Brook Farm and on to the lane. Stay on the lane as it winds left and up the hill to reach the road.

9. Turn right. Go down through the houses of Mugginton then go left at the public footpath sign, opposite Mugginton Primary School. Go between the houses then over the stile at the end and on to a green lane. Ignore footpaths to the left and stay on the lane. Where it emerges into the field, bear right to a wide gap in the right-hand boundary hedge. Cross the next field in the same direction, to a stile marked by an upright post on either side of a lane. Cross the lane and follow the direction of the footpath sign across the field. Go over the stream and the lane then over a stile by the side of Weston Underwood Water Works buildings. Follow the direction of the arrow up the field, past the buildings, then bear left to pick up a yellow arrow taking you left to a stile and steps down on to Cutler Lane and the parking area.

WALK 23
HARDWICK HALL

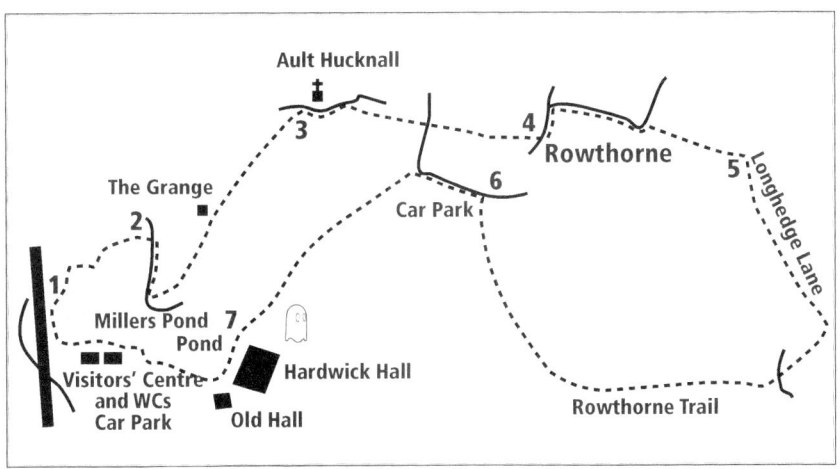

A very pleasant walk on tracks and trails through woods and fields with an abundance of ghosts at Hardwick Hall.

Distance: 7¼ miles

Grade: A

Parking: From J29 of the M1, take the A6175 following the sign for 'Hardwick Hall'. After ¼ mile turn left on Mill Lane, again signed 'Hardwick Hall'. Ignore the first sign to the left to 'Hardwick Hall' (after a mile) then, after passing under the motorway, turn left at the sign for 'Hardwick Park' (approx 2 miles from the A6175). Parking available on this access road or at the visitors' centre where the walk starts. Small charge. NB this is National Trust property.

Map Ref: SK 453640. Explorer 269 Chesterfield Map.

Pub Stop: None. WCs at visitors' centre at start of walk.

Route

1. With your back to the visitors' centre, walk straight ahead through the pay and display car park with the water on your right. Continue ahead to the end of the lake, staying at the side of the water. Follow the path round the end of the lake then go through a wooden gate and left at the T junction. The path climbs up through the wood. At the top, go ahead on to a road and turn right.

Hardwick Hall is haunted by an abundance of ghosts.

2. Go along the road, then 50 yards after reaching a cattle grid, at a left-hand hairpin bend, leave the road and turn left up the hillside on a broad path (unmarked). Continue straight ahead as the path climbs steadily. At the top, go through a wooden gate, past the buildings of The Grange on your left. Go ahead on the lane until you reach the road in Ault Hucknall.

3. Turn right.

The Church of St John the Baptist on your left is where Thomas Hobbes is buried. He is most famous as the author of one of the greatest books on political philosophy ever written, *Leviathan*, and for his philosophy based on a determinist mechanical system. He died in 1679 at Hardwick Hall, where his ghost has been seen.

Go down the road, then 50 yards after the Z-bend sign turn right over a stile. Take the left of two paths and go straight across two fields to reach a lane. Turn left and immediately right at the public footpath sign. Go ahead with the hedge on your left-hand side. In the following field, bear slightly right then walk parallel to the hedge on the left. Go over a stile and ahead to another stile and gate on to a lane.

4. Turn left. Then, on reaching a road on the right, turn right and go ahead for just under ½ mile. Where the road goes left, leave it to go straight ahead on a public footpath. Continue down the track until you reach a crossing of paths with a stile opposite.

5. Turn right. Stay on this lane (Longhedge Lane) for nearly ¾ mile then turn right (opposite the sign for Pleasley Pit Country Park), through a kissing gate with a yellow arrow sign on the side of a post for the 'Teversal Trail, Visitors' Centre and Rowthorne Trail.' Continue ahead for ¼ mile, then, just after crossing a bridge over a road and passing a notice board for 'Exploring the Rowthorne and Pleasley Trails', turn right over a stile. Go down a short slope, up the other side and left on to the Rowthorne Trail. Keep straight ahead on this pleasant path, ignoring any side paths, for 1½ miles until it reaches a car park. NB on the latter stages there is a parallel narrow path on the left which may be less muddy than the main trail and does emerge at the same point. At the car park entrance, go down a short lane to a road.

6. Turn left. Continue to a road junction. Turn left. At a building and gate saying no public access (this means for cars!) go through the pedestrian gate and ahead on the road to 'Hardwick Hall'.

In 1976 Mark Cresswell and Carol Rawlins were driving through the park on this road (which was allowed at that time) on their way to the Hardwick Inn. They manoeuvred around a fallen tree brought down in a recent storm then had to swerve to avoid a car hurtling towards them.

As they drove on through the park, Carol saw a figure among the trees with a shining white face, wearing a black monk's habit. She told Mark, and, though he said it must have been a tree stump, he turned the car around and drove back. The figure was still there, and it began to walk towards them, clearly seen in the headlights. At the last moment it veered off to the right, and they lost sight of it.

Later they told the landlady at the Hardwick Inn. Another couple in the pub overheard them and apologised, as it had been they who had nearly forced them off the road. They too had seen the monk and were trying to get away as fast as possible. The landlady told them that the phantom monk had been seen by six other people in the preceding week, including two policemen.

Go past the car and coach park to the front of the hall.

Hardwick Hall was built by Bess of Hardwick after the death of her fourth husband, George Talbot, Earl of Shrewsbury. By then she had become one of the wealthiest and most powerful women in England, second only to Elizabeth I. Her ghost is one of many said to haunt the hall.

Another spirit seen by many visitors is thought to be that of Christiana Bruce, young wife of the second Earl of Devonshire. An elderly man dressed in 18th-century clothes appears occasionally in the Great Hall, waiting patiently on a chair.

In the blue bedroom, which is said to get extremely cold, a teenage girl may be heard crying and indentations appear in the bed as though someone is lying on it.

The chapel and chapel landing is another haunted area. A woman has been sighted kneeling at the altar, and when the hall was closed a man was seen walking down the steps but disappeared when followed.

Other apparitions include a tall monk and a ghostly white cat that frequents the chapel landing and the gardens. There are also many reports of ghostly whisperings.

7. Bear right across the green and down between the buttress wall on the left and the fence on the right. Go through a wooden gate and turn right, heading for the ponds below. When you reach them, go right through a kissing gate between ponds then turn left at a broad track to walk with a fence on your right. Keep straight ahead through a gate to reach the visitors' centre and car parks.

WALK 24
ROWSLEY

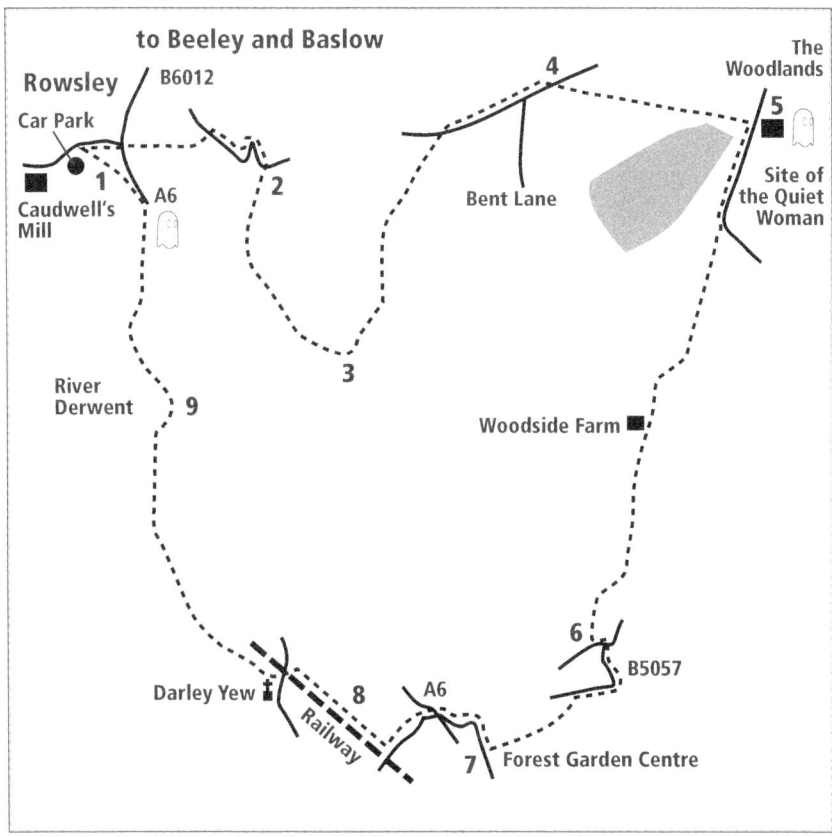

A great walk with a wonderful variety of scenery, taking you through fields, woods and moorland and returning by the River Derwent. It has panoramic views and, in late spring, it is made even more attractive by the bluebells, rhododendrons and wild garlic, while in August the heather provides a carpet of pink through which to walk.

Distance:	9 miles
Grade:	B
Parking:	Car park off Old Station Close, Rowsley. This is off the A6, opposite the sign for the Peak Village Factory Shopping.
Map Ref:	SK 258658. Outdoor Leisure White Peak Map.
Pub Stop:	Refreshments are available at the Forest Garden Centre, reached after six miles. It has a small licensed restaurant. Also in Rowsley there is Caudwell's Mill, open 10am to 6pm, available at the start and end of the walk for coffees, teas, light meals and cakes plus the Peacock and the Grouse and Claret pubs.

Route

1. From the car park, return to the A6, cross over and turn right. At the corner where the A6 goes right, cross the road to Beeley and Baslow and go up a footpath at the right-hand end of the shops. Go straight up with a wall on your right. Go over a stile and through a gap stile and ahead again, now with the wall on your left, continuing until you reach a road. Turn right. Go up the road, then after a left and right hairpin bend, take the public bridleway to Northwood on your right.

2. Continue on this very pleasant woodland path for about ¼ mile. Go through a stile at the side of an iron gate, cross a track to the left, through a wooden gate and then turn left up the track. Go through a small wooden gate, at the side of the 'Do Not Start a Fire' sign. Keep straight ahead for another ½ mile, ignoring a footpath to the left part way along, until you reach a T junction of paths at a stream.

3. Turn left. The path opens out with good views to the left and continues for ¾ mile until you reach a road. Turn right. After ¼ mile you pass Bent Lane on your right. Then about 150 yards further on, look for a gap stile on the right.

4. Go through it, and with your back to the stile bear left to 10 o'clock on a path through the heather, heading for the left-hand end of the trees on the skyline. When you reach the wood, go through the gap stile and ahead

with the trees on your left-hand side. Continue in the same direction across the field to a stile in the hedge to the left of the gate, on to a road.

The buildings opposite are on the site of an inn called the Quiet Woman, which dated back to Elizabethan times and is the haunt of a ghostly female arsonist.

It is said to be the daughter of the landlord, who was responsible for her father dying in a fire at the inn. The daughter was bad tempered and unwelcoming, which discouraged customers so the father supplemented their income by doing a bit of highway robbery on the side. One night his victim wounded him instead and headed for the inn. As he was tethering his horse, he saw the father arrive there and, in the light of a lantern held by the daughter, recognised his attacker. He gave a shout and dashed forward, but the daughter slammed the door shut.

The father, panicking, pushed past his daughter to conceal himself in the cellar, not realising he had knocked her to the floor and the lamp had ignited. When the daughter regained consciousness, she tried to put out the fire, but it spread rapidly and she had to watch her home burn down, unaware that her father was trapped inside. When her father's body was found in the blackened ruins, she became deranged, fleeing on to the moor where her body was later found.

Her ghost apparently lingered around the site of the inn, re-enacting the tragedy as the premises were rebuilt several times only to be repeatedly destroyed by fire. The inn was changed to a farm but again was razed to the ground. Even after the buildings were converted to a Country Club, it was again devastated by fire in 1966, and when the owner tried to rebuild it his caravan where he was temporarily lodging was also gutted by fire.

5. Turn right on the road. After 500 yards, where the road bends left, leave it to go straight ahead on a wide track through the trees. Continue on this pleasant path, bordered by rhododendrons in May/June. After ¾ mile, pass through Woodside Farm and continue on a paved lane. After passing

Site of the Quiet Woman Inn, haunted by a ghostly female arsonist.

Moorlands on the right, where the road goes left, leave it to go ahead on the track. It becomes deeply rutted, dropping down to eventually reach a road after ½ mile.

6. Turn left up the hill for 50 yards then turn right to go down Denacre Lane. Ignore Knab Road to the left and continue downwards. At the bottom of the lane, continue straight ahead on the road. When you reach the houses called Holt Gate and Holt Lodge on the left, turn left on the public footpath to Oddford Lane. At the end of the buildings, go ahead through a gap stile by an iron gate. Bear slightly right across the field, heading for a stile in the middle of the end hedge. Continue in the same direction across the following field to reach a paved path, where you turn right, emerging after a short distance on to a road at the Forest Garden Centre.

Refreshments are available in the garden centre.

7. Turn right. At the top of the hill, cross Warney Road and continue to the main road. Turn left. When you reach the A6, cross over it at the traffic lights, then go left following the sign for Darley Bridge, Wensley and Winster, going down Station Road. After 30 yards, turn right at the wrought-iron gates into the Whitworth Centre and Park. Take the first broad path to the left. Where the path forks, keep left. Continue to the end of the park then follow the path round to the right. At the pond, go around it with it on your right until you are facing up the park, then turn back 180 degrees on a short path to leave the park through a gate at the railway line. 8. Turn right.

Darley Dale Railway Station is to your left, and the ghost of a fireman is said to haunt the sheds here.

Stay on this path for ¼ mile to reach a road. Turn left over the railway crossing, down the road to the church.

The road to the left is Church Lane. In the 17th century it was known as Ghost Lane, the ghost being that of a Scottish pedlar who was robbed and murdered there. His ghost is seen near the large sycamore tree, 150 yards from the churchyard.

In the churchyard of Darley Dale Church is one of the largest yew trees in England, said to be over 2,000 years old (although some sources say it may be only 1,000). Whichever it is, its trunk is an amazing sight and it is well worth a visit. Around its base are commemorative tablets, depicting some of the most important battles of World War Two, erected soon after each event took place.

Turn right at the church (or if you've visited the Darley Yew, return to the road and turn left). Continue ahead at the signs for 'Abbey House' on a public footpath to Northwood. Go through the houses, through a gap stile and between the hedges. Cross over a step stile and straight ahead for four fields. At the end of the next field, go over the stile where the path joins the river and continue to a wide lane.

9. Turn left, signed 'Rowsley'. After 150 yards, cross a bridge over a stream at a sign saying 'We hope you have enjoyed your visit' and turn left on a concession path by the river. Stay on the path for 1 mile, to eventually reach Old Station Close and the car park.

At Rowsley Rail Station in 2004, members of the Society for Paranormal Research claim to have seen a man dressed in soldier's uniform, walking along the tracks, only to vanish when they went to investigate.

WALK 25
ELLASTONE/WOOTTON PARK

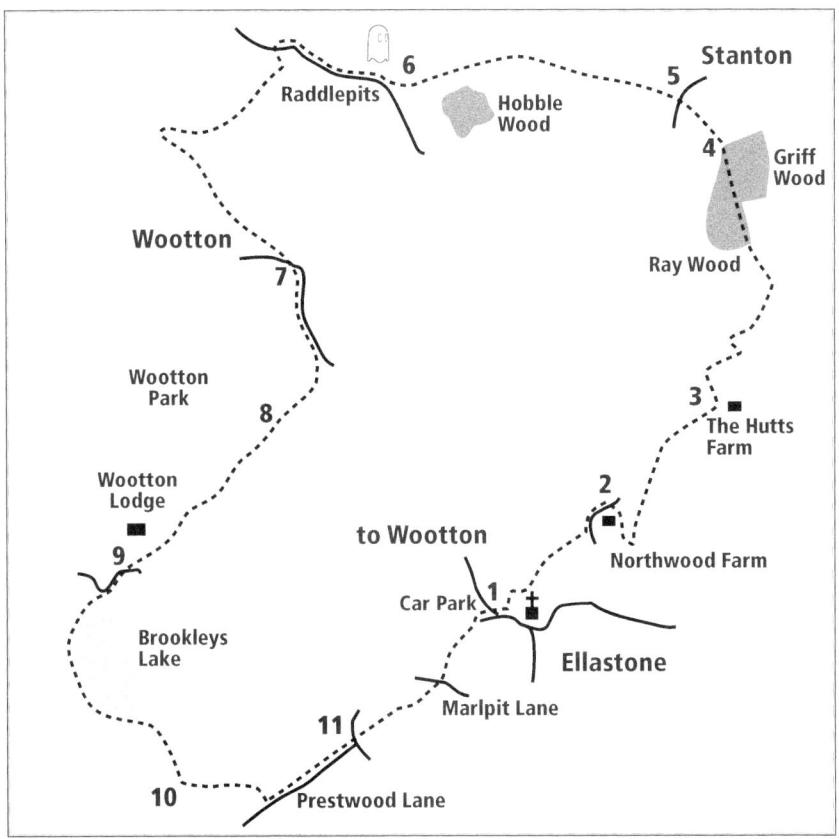

This has been described as a magical walk, with changes of scenery around every corner. It is set to the west of Ashbourne and has panoramic views taking in the Weaver Hills, the North Staffordshire Moorlands and the beautiful Wootton Park. While it is superb at any time of year, it is especially recommended in May/June for the rhododendrons and in autumn for the trees in the park.

Distance:	8½ miles
Grade:	C
Parking:	Upper Ellastone, off the B5032 SW of Ashbourne. In Ellastone, turn right at the sign for 'Wootton' then, after 100 yards, turn right again at the sign for parking. Car park is on left, at the end of Church Lane, opposite the church.
Map Ref:	SK 116435. Explorer 259 Derby Map.
Pub Stop:	None on walk. Duncombe Arms in Ellastone.

Ellastone is mentioned in the Domesday Book as Edelachestone or Elachestone. The Church of St Peter was built in the 16th century and has 1586 etched on the tower. Ellastone is the setting for 'Hayslope' in George Eliot's *Adam Bede*. The author's father spent the early part of his life working as a carpenter in the village.

Nearby are the ruins of Calwich Abbey, where the composer Handel stayed several times, and it is thought to have inspired some of his well-known pieces, such as the *Messiah* and *Water Music*.

Route

1. Leave the car park by the entrance and turn left, then after 50 yards turn right up the steps, into the churchyard through the gate. Go left, adjacent to the wall on the left, then left through a kissing gate and into a field. Bear left to a stile then go straight ahead across three fields. At the end of the third field, go over the stile on to a road. Turn left. Go past the buildings of Northwood Farm on your right, then turn right over a stone stile.

2. Cross a drive, go over a stile in a fence and down the slope to a gate. Bear right to a stile in the middle of the fence on the right. Continue to the corner and cross the wooden footbridge. Turn left, climb the slope and continue ahead on to a path, with the stone wall to your left. Bear right to a stile in the middle of the field then continue in the same direction to a stile at the end of the field. Bear right up the field to the corner of a small copse to the right, pass it and continue in the same direction up the hill, to reach a stile by a gate at the Hutts Farm.

3. Go ahead between the buildings and on to a lane, following it around a left-hand bend, then turn right over a stile in the fence on the right. Head down the field to the bottom left corner, cross the bridge and go up the slope on the far side to reach a grassy track. Turn right. When you reach the wood on your left, look for a footpath sign and stile into it. Go into the wood and ahead on a well-defined and, in parts, muddy track through the wood, eventually emerging in a field. Follow the direction of the arrow up the field, keeping a stone wall to your right for two fields. In the third field, head diagonally left to a stile (not the gate) in the far corner. Go over the stile into the wood (Ray Wood) and continue ahead with the wall on your left. After 10 yards, where the wall ends, continue in the same direction as before, do not go down the slope to the left. Stay on a path, weaving through bracken and woodland. This path becomes rather overgrown with bracken in late summer and autumn. Try to remain on a level as much as possible, not going down to the stream to your left, until eventually the path reaches a wall on your left. Continue by the wall/fence until you reach a stile. Go over the stile into a field and cross the stream ahead.

This is a pleasant place for a break, with rocks to sit on and a stream nearby.

4. Now cross the stream coming in from the left and bear right up the field with a wall to your right, curving gradually to the left as you climb the steep slope. Continue ahead where the field levels to reach a gate. Admire the view as you catch your breath, then go through the gate and across the next field with a wall to your left. Go through a gate into the following field, now with a wall to your right, then through the gate at the end on to a lane at Stanton.
5. Cross the lane and over the stile opposite and continue ahead with a wall to your right. Drop down into the hollow and up the other side to a stile to the right of the building. Go straight ahead up the field with a fence then a wall to your right, eventually reaching a gap stile on the right. Go through it, cross the corner of the next field and through another gap stile. Bear

right to 1 o'clock to a metal gate (possibly open) in the far boundary. Cross a track, bear right through a gap stile then down the field with the wall to your left. Go into the following field, now with the wall to your right, and bear left at the bottom to a footbridge over a stream (with Hobble Wood to your left). Keep going straight ahead, with a wall/fence to your left, climbing steadily up two very long fields. In the second field, when you reach a wood to your left, continue uphill by the side of it. Then, where it ends, go left around the top edge of it to reach a stile leading you on to a road (Raddlepits).

This is a good place for a lunch break, again with wonderful views.

To the north you have the North Staffordshire Moorlands and the scene of your ghost story. It is said that a family who lived on the moor were tried and executed for murder when it was discovered that they supplemented their diet by feeding off the flesh of those lost on the moor. For years after their deaths, sounds could be heard of them chasing their victims over the desolate moor land. No date is given for this gruesome tale and I'm fairly sure they don't do it anymore, so enjoy your lunch!

The North Staffordshire Moorlands are haunted by a man-eating family.

6. Turn right up the road, then after 300 yards, at a cattle grid, go over a stile to the left at a public footpath sign. Go ahead, following the wall to the left, and through a second stile. The path drops down and curves to the right, following the contour of the hill, for about ½ mile, with a wall on your left. Pass a wooden gate, then after 100 yards go left through a gap stile. Go down the field with wall to your left. Halfway down the field, turn left over a stile. Follow the direction of the arrow (on top of a post) across a field to a second arrow by a gate. Continue to follow its direction over the next field and ahead on to a lane. Go down the lane to reach a road.

7. Turn left into the village of Wootton.

The inhabitants formerly described this place as 'Wootton under Weaver, where God came never'.

Where the road bends right, follow it round and down the hill. About 200 yards after the end of the houses, turn right through a gate at a public footpath sign. Go up the path and straight ahead in the field, joining a wall on your right, to pick up an arrow sign, then drop down to a stile in a fence. Turn right, and when you reach the wood go through a gate in the fence. Go through the wood, following the arrow signs, gradually descending and then over a stile at the bottom into Wootton Park.

8. Cross the road and go straight ahead, adjacent to the fence/rhododendron wood to your right. At the bottom, cross the road and continue in the same direction, bearing right across the park. Go past a water trough to arrows on a tree and ahead to a road. Cross the road and continue ahead in the same direction to reach a wall. Go ahead, keeping the wall to your right. At the end of the wall, go through a gate to your right, then left, to continue in the same direction as before, on a narrow path through shrubs and trees, following the arrow signs. Emerging into an open area, bear right following the arrow sign. Then, just before the buildings, bear right down to the road, picking up an arrow sign on a post.

The impressive building to your right is Wootton Lodge, a 16th-century house owned by the Bamford family (JCB Excavators).

Cross the road and follow the direction of the arrow, with Wootton Lodge to your right. When you reach the rhododendron bushes, you will find another arrow sign pointing to the right, taking you between them. Go down this path, through the door, emerging eventually on to a road.

9. Turn right. Go down the hill, then where the road bends right leave it, at a public footpath sign, and go through a gap stile. Keep ahead on a path through the trees to reach a lake. Turn right, then after 50 yards turn left, across the road and down a footpath opposite. Follow the path to reach a road and keep ahead with the lake to your left. At the far end of the lake, where the road goes right and left, cross over and go on to a path between the roads, going left through the trees. Cross a bridge and up into the woodland. Keep straight ahead. When you reach the road, cross over and go ahead through the trees, following the signs. At the end, turn left back to the road.

10. Cross the road, go over a stile by the (open) gateway and continue ahead to a stile in a fence. Bear left to another stile in a fence. Turn right and walk with the fence on your right. When you reach a building, go right through the gate and down the grassy path. At a T junction, turn right then left at the next T junction (Prestwood Lane). At the end of the lane, at a third T junction, go straight across and over a stile into a field.

11. Follow the direction of the footpath sign up the field. Where it levels out, bear right to a stile in the right-hand hedge. Go over a stile and ahead, then at the corner head diagonally left across the field to an iron gate in the far corner. Go over a stile (to the left of the gate) on to a lane (Marlpit Lane), turn right and almost immediately left over a stile in the hedge. Go straight down the field to a stile in the bottom left corner. Continue in the same direction in the next field with the hedge on your left. In the following field, bear right to a stile. Cross the brook and bear right again in the next field to reach the main road. Turn left then right at a footpath sign. Bear right to a second stile and along a narrow path to reach the car park.

WALK 26
RENISHAW

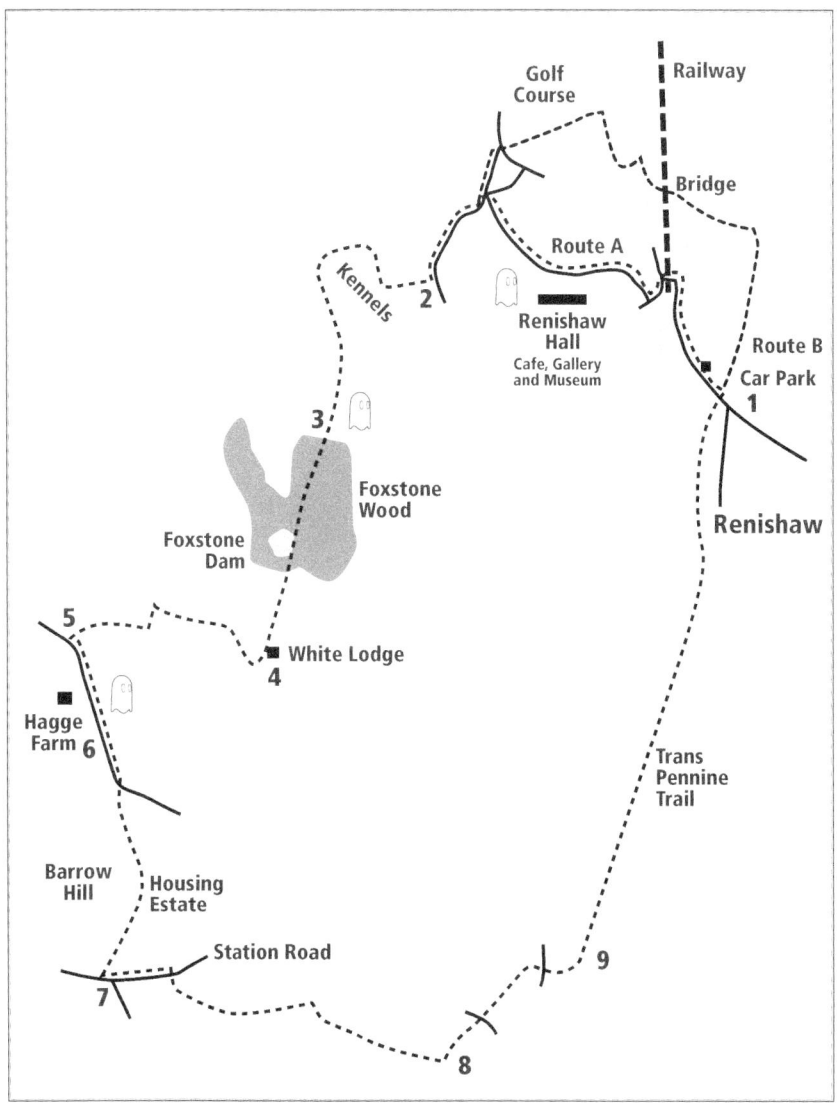

Golf Course

Railway

Bridge

Route A

Kennels

2

Renishaw Hall
Cafe, Gallery and Museum

Route B
Car Park
1

3

Foxstone Wood

Foxstone Dam

Renishaw

White Lodge

4

5

Hagge Farm 6

Trans Pennine Trail

Barrow Hill

Housing Estate

Station Road

7

9

8

On this easy walk in the north of Derbyshire you have a choice at the start. Between April and the end of September there is the added interest of walking through Renishaw Park and visiting Renishaw Hall (called Derbyshire's best-kept secret), with its Italianate Gardens, Sitwell Museum, Galleries and Lakeside Walks. Between October and March the walk takes you to the north of the hall through attractive woodland.

NB Broxhill Wood at Renishaw is awash with bluebells in late spring and is situated to the right of the hall when facing it. Both walks start from the same place and join at Section 2. They are on good paths and tracks, although some parts may be overgrown in late summer.

Distance: 8½ miles if visiting Renishaw Hall or 9 miles otherwise

Grade: A/B

Parking: From junction 30 of the M1, take the A6135 road to Renishaw. The car park is reached after nearly two miles. After passing the B6419 to the left, the access road is down a narrow lane just before the Sitwell Arms (down the right-hand side when facing it). There is a small car park on the Trans Pennine Trail (not signed).

Map Ref: SK 445782. Explorer 269 Chesterfield Map.

Pub Stop: None. If visiting Renishaw Hall there are refreshments available at the Gallery Café at Renishaw Hall. There are also WCs in the courtyard.

NB tours of the hall are only by special arrangement, but the gardens, museum, galleries and gallery café are open from April to the end of September from 10.30am to 4.30pm on Thursdays, Fridays, Saturdays, Sundays and Bank Holidays. There are occasional special events in the remaining part of the year. However, it is best to double check opening dates and times on the website www.sitwell.co.uk if wanting to include it in the walk.

Route A goes through Renishaw Park but see opening times above. Otherwise use Route B.

1. Leave the car park by the access road to reach the main (A6135) road. Turn right and continue up the road. Cross a bridge over the river. Then, just after you cross a bridge over the railway, turn left at a 'No Entry' sign for Renishaw Hall and walk up the access road. At a junction, where an old entrance is to the left, go right, not to the lakes, and walk up the road to the hall.

In the 19th century, a ghost once woke a female guest at Renishaw Hall by kissing her three times. The lady jumped up and turned on the light, only to find her locked bedchamber empty. This apparition has been called the Little Boy in Pink, and it is thought to be a sickly child who died in 1726 at the age of 13. He seems to like to snuggle up to lady guests in a certain bedroom and give them three cold kisses.

After a wall of this bedroom had been knocked down and incorporated into a new staircase, Lady Ida Sitwell saw a grey-haired woman in a white cap and crinoline glide along the corridor and vanish at the spot where the old door to the haunted room had been.

Renishaw Hall, where you may be woken by three cold ghostly kisses.

Another guest is said to have watched a woman dressed in blue and white dart down a corridor, her arms outstretched, then promptly vanish as she reached the staircase. An empty coffin, though with signs of previously having held a body, was found concealed under the bedroom at the time of the renovation of the staircase.

With your back to the hall and the access to the galleries, museum and café to your left, bear left to leave the park by an access road going down the hill (north east for those with a compass!). When you reach the main road, turn left. Continue along the road past Southgate to the right. Climb the hill. Ignore the first public footpath to the right, then turn right at the public bridleway sign.

Route B (excluding Renishaw Hall)
1. From the car park, leave by a track opposite the entrance, going up the slope adjacent to the purple notice board for the Trans Pennine Trail to your left. Continue on the trail until you reach a wooden bench and a crossing of paths. Turn left and go down the slope to a lane. Turn right, then after 30 yards go left through a kissing gate into Birley Wood. Go ahead on a pleasant woodland path.

Go through another kissing gate, then beyond it, where there is a choice of paths, take the one to the left down the hill. Pass through the white-painted kissing gate and cross the bridge over the railway. Go over the stile and bear right across the field. Go over a stream then bear left in the field to a footbridge over a river. On the far side, where the path divides, go right. Go right again to pick up an arrow on a post, directing you down the side of the golf course, with the course to your left.

When you reach a second footbridge on your right, turn left to cross the golf course (taking care not to interfere with golfers). On the far side of the course, go on to a narrow path to reach a road. Bear right and almost immediately left on Park Hill. Go past the entrance to Renishaw Hall and continue along the road, passing Southgate to the right. Climb the hill. Ignore the first public footpath to the right then turn right at the public bridleway sign.

Routes join here.

2. Keep ahead. When you come to a corner, go right, not into the field. At the next junction turn left. Continue on a rutted lane. When you reach a road, keep straight ahead. Pass Hornthorpe Kennels then turn immediately left and go up a path by the side of it (not signposted). At the end of the kennels' fencing, go left then right to continue in the same direction as before.

The path carries on between walls and may be overgrown in places, especially in late summer. In this case it is possible to leave it and walk adjacent to it in the field to the right, returning when it improves in its latter stages. Continue ahead until you reach a wood.

In 1986 Geoff Cooper was walking his dog Shelley in this area. As he neared the wood, he glanced behind and saw a young man about 50 yards behind him. He entered the wood, presuming that the lad was going to Renishaw Park Pit. As the youth came closer, he noticed that he was dressed in very old fashioned clothes and was wearing a flat cap and was carrying a snap tin.

By this time Shelley was acting very strangely, walking under Geoff's feet. She was straining at the lead and was generally unsettled, which was most unlike her. As the young man came up to his shoulder, Geoff turned to speak to him but there was no one there.

Although he felt no fear, he was intrigued by the incident and was sure that he had seen a ghost. His research lead him to an old lady who had also had unexplained experiences at the same spot. She told him that there had once been an old tramway in that area and a death associated with it. Formerly a sceptic, Geoff is sure that he saw the ghost of a young miner killed on the tramway many years before.

3. Go into Foxstone Wood and keep straight ahead, ignoring any side paths. Pass a lake to your right, Foxstone Dam, which is a good place for a coffee break. Leave the wood and go ahead on a clear path and then on to a broad lane. Pass some buildings (White Lodge) then turn right through a wooden gate at a sign for 'Bridleway 16'.

4. Walk adjacent to the hedge on your left. Pass an opening, then where the boundary bends to the left follow it round. Continue in the same direction in the next field. At the end of it, go through a wooden gate (open) and straight ahead. When you meet a hedge, turn left, following the bridleway sign, to walk with the hedge on your right. At the end of this hedge, turn right through a wooden gate at a public bridleway sign, though not indicating your direction! Stay adjacent to the left-hand boundary to eventually emerge on to a road.

5. Turn left. After 300 yards you reach Hagge Farm on your right.

Hagge Farm, formerly known as The Hagge, was once famous for its Mandrake Tree, an oak guarded by a fearsome ghost and worshipped by druids. The tree was said to scream and bleed if its branches were cut and was also said to speak with the voice of prophetic doom. Unfortunately, after existing since the time of Henry VIII, it succumbed to a terrible gale in December 1883 and was blown down.

The house is reputed to be haunted by a White Lady. This is thought to be the ghost of Sarah Harrington, wife of Colonel Culpepper. When The Hagge was occupied by a Mr Cranshaw, an Irish visitor to it enquired at breakfast whether the lady in white would be joining them as he had passed her on the stairs the previous night.

6. Continue down the road. After another 400 yards, on a left-hand bend, turn right at a public footpath over a stile in the hawthorn hedge. Follow the direction of the sign across the field to reach a stile emerging on to a short lane. Ignore a stile opposite leading on to scrubland. Instead, bear slightly left to go into the field to walk on a wide cart track with a hedge on your right. Where the track bends to the left, continue straight ahead to keep a fence on your right, emerging on to a road by a housing estate. Continue down past the houses until you reach a junction.

7. Turn left on the first main road, not the one going under the bridge. (The road you want is Station Road, although the sign is hard to spot!) Go past the Barrow Pub (vacant at this time) and Barrow Hill Memorial Club. Go up the hill then turn right at the public footpath sign for the Trans Pennine Trail and

Chesterfield Canal. Pass the disused Methodist Chapel then ahead on a tarmac lane.

Where the path divides, stay adjacent the right-hand iron fence. Cross the bridge over the old railway and continue ahead, now with a hedge on your left, following the yellow arrow sign. Continue ahead between fences and go through a tunnel. When you reach a junction of paths, take the left-hand one with an iron fence on your left, not up a broad slope. Go up a flight of steps and down the other side. Cross a modern footbridge over the River Rother. On the far side, bear left to emerge on to a broad track.

8. Turn left. When you come to a road, cross straight over staying on the Trans Pennine Trail to Renishaw. Go under a bridge beneath the road. Follow the sign for the Trans Pennine Trail. At a signpost, turn left towards Renishaw. Follow the Trans Pennine Trail arrow sign at the next gap stile, ignoring Cuckoo Way to the right just after this. Turn right, following the Renishaw signpost at the next junction on to Trans Pennine Trail.

9. Stay on the Trans Pennine Trail for two miles. Pass under a bridge beneath the road and keep straight ahead. Go down a short hill and into the car park.

Foxstone Wood, where you may meet a ghostly miner.

WALK 27 AND 28
DALE ABBEY

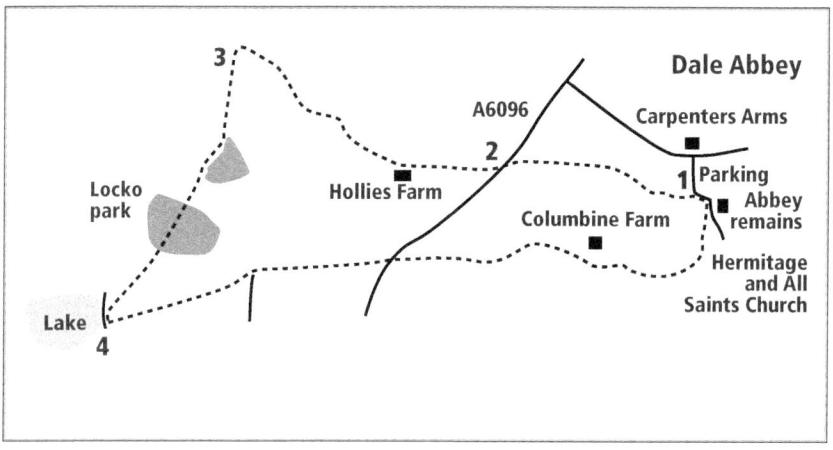

A most attractive walk in an area full of interest. It is on good paths through a variety of scenery. It may be combined with Walk 28 to form a figure of eight longer walk.

Distance: 5 miles

Grade: A

Parking: On a road called The Village (opposite the Carpenters Arms Pub) in Dale Abbey.

Map Ref: SK 437393. Explorer 260 Nottingham Map.

Pub Stop: The Carpenters Arms in Dale Abbey. Open lunchtimes and evenings. The Gateway Christian Centre on The Village serves light refreshments on Sundays and spring and summer bank holidays 2.30 to 5pm and is open at other times by arrangement.

Route

1. Go down to the bottom of the road called The Village and turn right on to Tattle Hill.

The name is thought to be derived from the tittle-tattle of neighbours. Note the thatched, rather up-market 'cow shed' on the left, last used in the 1940s.

The Legend of the Outlaw

There is a legend associated with the founding of the abbey, which concerns a notorious outlaw called Uthlagus, who, together with his villainous band, would prey on travellers between Nottingham and Derby.

One day, when he was resting to the west of the village, he fell asleep on the hill of Lyndrick and had a strange vision. It was of a golden cross rising from the valley below, from the place where the abbey was later built, high into the sky, and its arms spread as far as the eye could see. He saw men coming to worship there from all the nations on earth.

When he awoke he told his fellow robbers that it was a holy place and that he would no longer pursue a life of crime. He returned to the dale and sought out the hermit who lived there, and he devoted his life, from that time, to meditation and prayer.

Go over a stile by a gate then turn right up the field, with the hedge on your right, and over a stile at the top. Turn left on a broad path. When you emerge into a field, bear slightly right to a stile in the middle of the far hedge. In the next two fields, walk with the hedge on your right. Keep straight ahead in a third field to reach the road (A6096).

2. Turn left. After 100 yards, turn right at the sign for 'Hollies Farm', following the public bridleway sign (not the footpath sign). Keep ahead on a paved road. Continue down the drive of the farm and pass through the delightfully converted buildings. Go through a small wooden gate at the side of an iron one and straight ahead through a gap stile, following the yellow arrow sign across the field, then turn right on to a lane. Stay on it at a right-hand bend, ignoring the stile to the left. Where the track enters a field, continue ahead with the hedge to your left. At a (broken) wooden gate, bear left, keeping adjacent to the hedge on the left.

3. Go through a second wooden gate then almost immediately left through an iron gate. Ignoring a broad track to the left, bear right to walk across the field with the hedge on the right-hand side, heading for a copse. Go ahead for two fields then cross the stile and continue in the same direction for two further fields, but now with the hedge on your left. In a second field, follow the fence round to the right then over a footbridge into a third field. Follow the direction of the arrow signs across the field. Go through an iron kissing gate and straight ahead in a wood. On leaving the wood, go down the field, heading for the road.

This is Locko Park, which has been the ancestral home of the Drury-Lowe family since 1747.

4. On reaching the road, turn sharp left. Continue ahead, passing two houses. Just beyond the second, where you emerge on to a lane, go ahead down a short path to a main road (A6096). Cross over and up the footpath on the other side. When you reach a lane, keep straight ahead. At Columbine Farm, go up to the right. Pass through a gate and bear slightly left on a clear path, with a hedge to your left. Continue in the same direction when you reach a gravelled path, go through a gate and straight ahead into woodland. Go through an iron gate and across a field, with a hedge to your left. When you arrive at a house, bear left down the path.

The building to the right is a farmhouse and attached to the back of it is All Saints Church. This is probably one of the smallest churches in the country, measuring just 26ft by 25ft. It stands on the site of an earlier chapel, built by a hermit, who, following a visitation by the Virgin Mary, gave up his life as a baker in Derby. He travelled to Depedale (as Dale Abbey was then known) and carved out the cave in Hermits Wood.

Many years after, the hermitage and chapel became the infirmary and chapel for the abbey. A low balcony and connecting door allowed the

patients to see from a prone position. When, in later years, the house next door became an inn called the Blue Bell, the connecting door from the church was said to lead from salvation to damnation.

It lays claim to being Derbyshire's first cathedral and became the Gretna Green of the Midlands as licences were issued for weddings without banns having to be read.

Its curious interior holds a wealth of interest, from its box pews to its beautifully-carved leaning pulpit.

There is a service every Sunday from 3 until 4pm. Visitors are made very welcome, and it is well worth the effort to attend, both to view the interior and to experience worship in this unique church.

Continue down the path to the gate at the bottom. Pass a footpath to the right. After a few yards, you reach a second footpath at a stile by a gate. This is the start of Walk 28.

To return to parking, follow the lane as it winds left and right, then turn right back on to The Village.

All Saints Church, Dale Abbey.

163

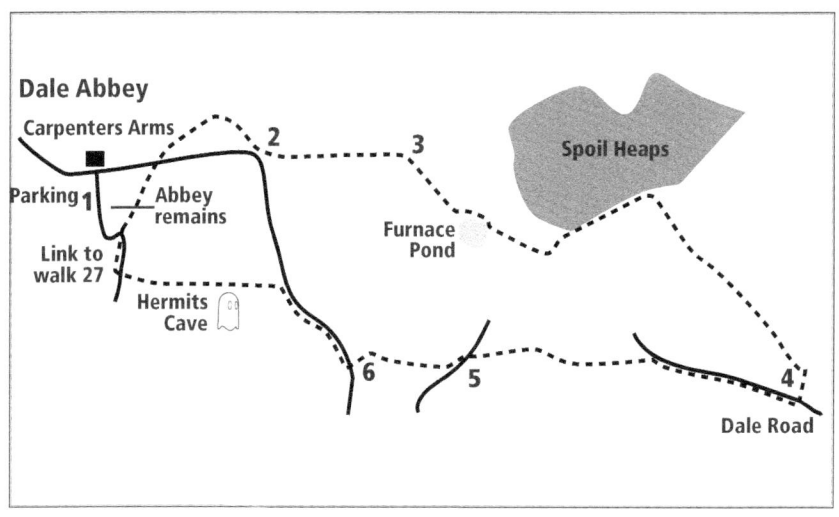

This is the second of two enjoyable walks in this interesting area. It has a variety of scenery and good views. It may be combined with Walk 27 to make a longer walk.

Distance: 4 miles

Grade: A

Parking: On a road called The Village (opposite the Carpenters Arms Pub) in Dale Abbey. Will accommodate a few cars if parked with consideration to residents' drives. The Carpenters Arms may allow parking if returning for refreshments there. Also see note in Section 6 about additional parking in the lay-by at map ref SK 443383.

Map Ref: SK 437393. Explorer 260 Nottingham Map.

Pub Stop: The Carpenters Arms in Dale Abbey is open lunchtimes and evenings. The Gateway Christian Centre on The Village serves light refreshments on Sundays and spring and summer bank holidays from 2.30 to 5pm and is open at other times by arrangement.

Route

1. From The Village, go down to the bottom of the road and turn left. Follow the road round to left, then where it bends right go over a stile by a gate at a public footpath sign.

This is where Walk 27 may be joined to this one.

Go ahead in the field, then after 10 yards go left round the back of a house and over a second stile. Continue walking by the hedge on the left.

To the left is the 40ft-high chancel window, which is all that remains of St Mary's Abbey. This was completed in about 1250 and was a house of Pre-monstratensian Canons, called the White Canons because of the colour of their habits. Excavations have shown that the abbey's transepts were 100ft in length, with a cloister of 85ft square and a nave of unknown length. It remained until the Dissolution of the Monasteries under Henry VIII in 1538, when it was almost completely demolished.

Continue ahead into the next field, then bear diagonally right to the corner. Go over a stile, then after a few yards go left over a second stile in the hedge to the road. Cross over the road and over a stile on the far side and follow the direction of an arrow across the field. Go into the next field, then go diagonally right to a stile, just past the building, in the right-hand boundary hedge. Go down a narrow path to reach a lane.

2. Turn left. Go over the ford. Where the lane bends left, leave it to go ahead between the fences. Go straight across the field. Go over a stile on the far side and continue ahead between the fence and the hedge.

3. Turn right on to a bridleway. Go over three stiles by the gates. When you reach a pond, bear left to keep the water to your right.

Furnace Pond is the flooded remains of an old ironstone mine. In 1905 three people were saved from drowning here by John Padgett.

The remains of Dale Abbey.

Continue straight ahead in the field and pass the end of the trees. Pass the mound of the spoil heaps to the left, then turn left to a stile by an iron gate, heading for the chimney in the distance. Go straight ahead with the hedge/poplars to your left. Two thirds of the way down the field (where you reach a stile in wooden fencing to the left), turn right across the field and on to a path. Go over the stile and straight across the field. On the far side, go up the hill, over a stile and straight ahead. Continue in the same direction in the next field, cutting across the corner, then over a stile and continue ahead, with the hedge on your right. Go into the next field, then after 50 yards turn right at a wide gap (unmarked) and walk down the field with the hedge on your left to reach a road (Dale Road).

4. Turn right. Stay on the road until you reach Grove Cottage on the left. Turn left here, over a stile at a public footpath sign. Go through the iron gate and diagonally across the field to the corner. Go over a stile and straight ahead, then follow the path as it climbs and then contours to the right. Go over two stiles and ahead between the hedge and woodland. When you emerge in a field, follow the direction of the arrow sign, bearing left for two fields. Cross the corner of the following field, over a stile on to a road.

5. Turn left. Just before you reach a house on the left, turn right over a stile and follow the direction of the public footpath sign across a field. Cross the corner of the next field to reach a road.

6. Turn right (Woodpecker Hill).

There is a large lay-by here with additional parking. If parking here, start the walk by facing the lay-by and go right to the public footpath and bridleway signs (opposite the road signposted to Stanton-by-Dale). Turn left at a wooden gate.

Pass the lay-by, then turn left at the public footpath and bridleway signs, through a wooden gate. Go ahead on a clearly defined path then through a wooden gate to enter Hermit's Wood. After 10 yards, go up the steps on the left to visit the hermit's cave.

Hermit's Cave, Dale Abbey, is haunted by a monk.

In about 1130 a Derby baker had a vision that told him he must go to Depedale (now Dale Abbey) and spend his life in prayer there. Not knowing where it was, he nevertheless started on his journey. His footsteps guided him to the village of Stanley, where he heard a woman telling her daughter to take some calves to Depedale. He followed the girl there and found a desolate marshy place. He carved out a cave in the sandstone and lived the life of a recluse.

The owner of the land, Ralph Fitz Geremund, saw the smoke from his fire one day and went to drive him from his land. But he was filled with compassion when he heard the hermit's story and bestowed upon him the tithes from Borrowash Mill. This allowed the hermit to build a small chapel on the site of the present church.

Hermit's Wood is believed to be haunted by a monk who committed suicide many centuries ago. Strange banging noises have been heard and people have reported feelings of not being alone or of being watched. His apparition is said to be seen standing under the arch late at night.

Continue past the hermit's cave and go down the steps, to return to the main track. Go left and continue through the wood. When you leave it, go ahead then right on the gravel path past the farmhouse on the right with All Saints Church attached. (See Walk 27 for details.)

Go down to the bottom and through the gate on to the lane. Follow it round to the left then turn right on to the parking area on The Village.

WALK 29
SUTTON SCARSDALE

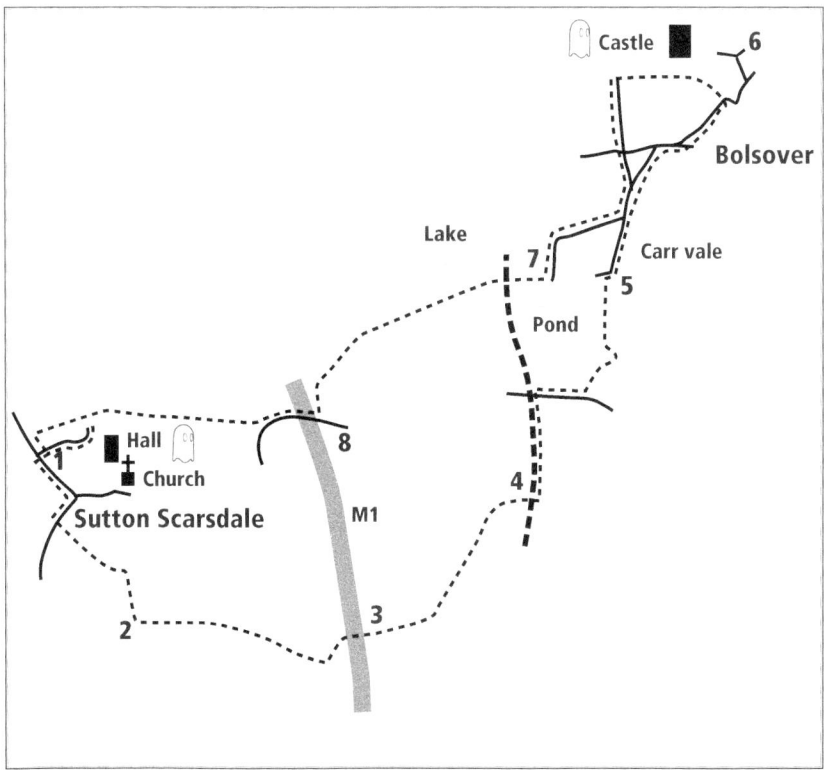

This walk, which crosses the Vale of Scarsdale, encompasses the wonderfully-atmospheric ruins of Sutton Scarsdale Hall on its lofty hilltop and the fairy tale splendour of Bolsover Castle on the other side of the valley, both with more than their share of ghostly inhabitants.

Distance: 7 miles

Grade: B. Steep ascent up to Bolsover Castle and steady climb on return.

Parking: Sutton Scarsdale Hall. From J29 of the M1, take the A6175. After ¾ mile turn right to Sutton Scarsdale and follow the signs to the village. Turn right in the village at the sign for the hall. NB the car park is open 10am to 6pm 1 April to 30 September and 10am to 5pm 1 October to 31 March

Map Ref: SK 442681. Explorer 269 Chesterfield Map.

Pub Stop: The café at Bolsover Castle serves light refreshments.

Bolsover Castle is haunted by many ghosts, who may slap, tickle or tug your clothes.

Route

1. From the hall, return up the access road to the main road. Turn left. Follow the road round to the right at the junction, then after 50 yards turn left at the footpath sign and go down the field, with the hedge on your left. Go past the pylon, down a slope and across a footbridge. Go left and up to a stile. Cross the field, with a fence on your left, to reach a lane.

2. Turn left. Go down the lane to the bottom and over a stile. Turn left on to the track and continue ahead under the bridge below the M1.

3. On the far side, go straight ahead in a field to a gap in the hedge, then go left across the corner of the second field to a stile. Follow the direction

of the arrow sign in a third, large field, heading directly for Bolsover Castle on the skyline, and continue in the same direction in the fourth field. Cross a footbridge and follow the arrow signs across two more fields to reach the Stockley Trail.

4. Turn left. When you reach a road, turn right. After about 500 yards, turn left on a green lane with a metal barrier at the entrance (unmarked by sign). Follow the lane as it bends left. When the lane ends, go into the field ahead and turn right, to walk with the hedge on your right. Continue ahead until you reach a lane.

5. Turn right. Keep straight ahead, passing a post office to your right, up Main Street (this is Carr Vale). Keep ahead at a junction (i.e. not on Chapel Road). Bolsover Castle can be seen ahead. At a mini roundabout, go right, then go left up Castle Hill (there is a postbox on the right-hand corner of the road).

This is a steep hill. Partway up there is a seat (on a Z-bend, with the footpath to your left). Anyone unable or not wishing to go to the top could remain here, as the walk returns to this point and takes the footpath.

At the top, go ahead on Castle Street to reach the entrance to Bolsover Castle on your left.

If you visit the castle you may find yourself being pinched or pushed along by one of its many supernatural presences, and many visitors have reported being slapped, tickled or having their clothes tugged.

On the terrace, Civil War soldiers may march up and down or you may hear the sound of tramping feet or phantom horses trotting.

In the fountain garden, a grey lady appears through an archway and ghostly knights parade around the thick wall.

If you have children with you, a small boy may join you in this area, taking your child's hand.

In the 'little castle' Sir William Cavendish's favourite place was the

Elysium Room, and here people sometimes smell pipe smoke. A member of staff who joked about Sir William being a bit of a ladies' man was pushed on the stairs by some entity and hurt her ankle.

The wooden-floored room, last occupied by Mrs Robbins, a housekeeper in the 19th century, provides the most reports. Visitors sometimes have difficulty entering or exiting this room as the housekeeper has a habit of locking the door. They also experience strange mists and breathing difficulties and a feeling of claustrophobia.

The kitchen is also a very haunted area, and there is said to be a hollow space below it, which was once a church or a dungeon, although it has never been opened.

A medium staying the night at the castle reported many happenings, including one of the most frightening stories. She saw a young woman hurry through the kitchen with a bundle in her arms and go into the side room housing the ovens. She glanced around then opened the oven door and thrust the bundle inside. As she did this a baby screamed. Then, as the screams faded, so did the ghostly woman and the baby that she must have burnt to death so many years ago.

6. When you leave the castle, turn right and return the way you came, going straight ahead at the corner down the hill. Go round a right-hand bend, then at the next left-hand bend leave the road to go right on to a public footpath. Where the path divides, take the left hand one to go down the field, with the hedge on your left (there is a wonderful view at this point). At the bottom, bear left on to a path. Go ahead through a kissing gate. At a second kissing gate, turn left on to a road, to walk with houses on your right. At the main road, go straight ahead on Chapel Road. At the next road, turn right and continue down until you reach Charlesworth Street. Turn right, then turn left on Sutton Hall Road. Go down to the end of the road and ahead over a footbridge.

7. Turn right and go past a pond to reach the Stockley Trail. Go straight over the trail, following the sign for 'Sutton Scarsdale Hall'. Go over a footbridge and left on a path, until you are level with the end of the lake.

Sutton Scarsdale Hall is haunted by a legless phantom, a grey figure and strange floating lights.

Turn right to a stile at the right-hand end of a hedge beyond the lake. Follow the direction of the arrow across the field, heading directly for Sutton Scarsdale Hall on the horizon. In the following field, continue in the same direction, keeping the ruined buildings to the right. On the far side, turn left to reach a road.

8. Turn right and cross the M1. Go up the road, then just before the first house turn right at a footpath sign and go up the field with the fence on your left. When the fence ends, keep ahead on a broad track to reach the moat of the hall (this denies access to the hall very effectively!). Follow the moat round to the right and keep ahead when you reach the buildings. Continue straight on through the works and up the drive (not too close to the guard dog on the right – thankfully chained!) to exit up a short path on to the road. Turn left then left again at the access road to the hall and go back to the car park.

If it is now late afternoon, it may be the best time to sample the atmosphere of this once great hall, thought at one time to be the finest in Derbyshire. Built in 1724 for Nicholas the 4th Earl of Scarsdale, its interior was ornate and its gardens lavish. It is worth walking around to the front of the mansion to see the view it commanded.

For many years there have been tales of it being haunted. This empty shell, with its brooding silence broken only by the cawing of crows (thought to carry the spirit of humans to the afterlife), certainly feels extremely eerie. There have been sightings of a legless ghost wearing a white hood with only slits for eyes. People have also seen a grey figure walking towards the back of the church. Other reports are of phantom footsteps and voices, fleeting shadows and strange floating white lights at night.

WALK 30
STAUNTON HAROLD RESERVOIR

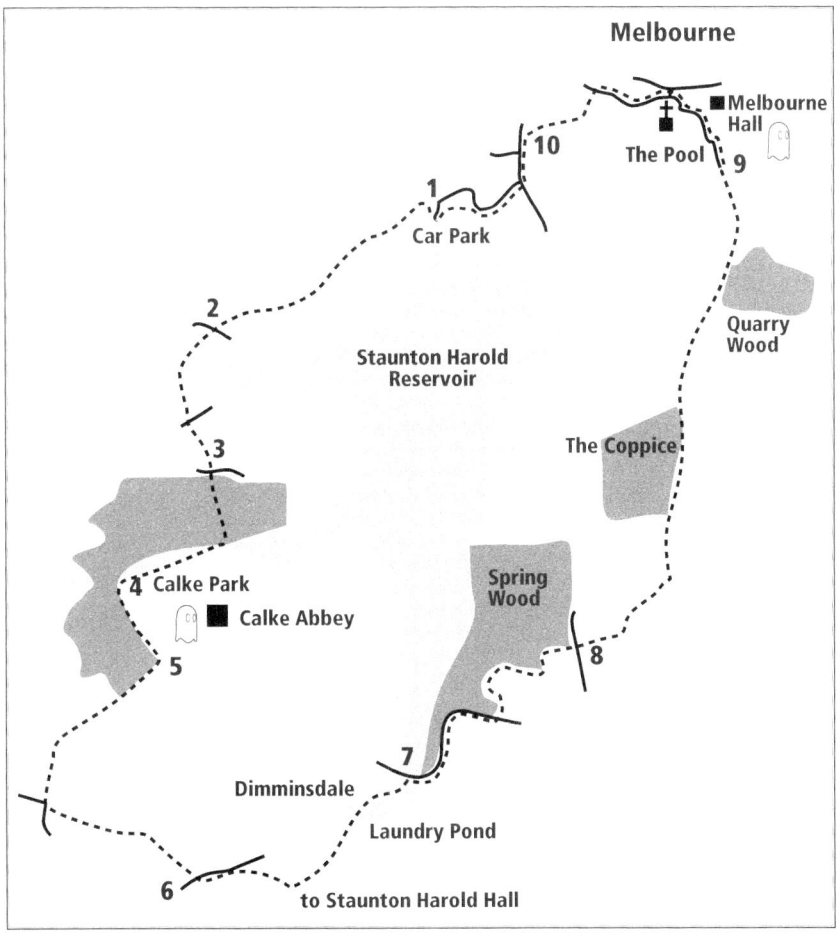

A delightful walk with a wide variety of scenery, starting from Staunton Harold Reservoir. It visits Calke Park, returning through Melbourne via an attractive mix of fields, woods, lakes and pools.

Distance: 8 miles

Grade: A/B

Parking: Staunton Harold Reservoir. Access is via Calke Road off the B587 near Melbourne. NB this is a pay and display car park – £1.50 at time of writing. There is also a visitors' centre and WCs.

Map Ref: SK 378244. Explorer 245 The National Forest Map.

Pub Stop: None. Refreshments may be had at Melbourne Hall Tea Rooms. NB between November and March it only opens at weekends. At other times, you are advised to check first. Tel 01332 864224. Melbourne Hall is open every afternoon in August only (except Mondays). Gardens open April to September in afternoons on Wednesdays, Saturdays and Sundays. www.melbournehall.com. Tel 01332 862502.

Route

1. From the car park, return up the access road to the tower. Bear left to a public footpath and go across the field, following the direction of the sign and line of telegraph poles. On the far side, bear left to walk with the hedge on your right. Go over a stile and ahead, with the hedge on your right, for three fields, ignoring the path to the left in the third. In the fourth field, go straight across, then on the far side bear right, to walk now with the hedge on your left. Go over a stile and along the path by the wood and ahead, again with the hedge on your left. Follow the direction of the arrow across the next two fields.

2. Cross a lane, go over the stile opposite and follow the direction of the arrow, bearing right down the field. Go over the footbridge and straight ahead up the following field. Ignore the stile to right. At the edge of the field, go left on to the path, to walk with the wall on your right. Pass the open gateway and continue with the fence on your right. Where the path emerges into the field, go straight ahead to a stile in the fence. Go over the stile, cross the lane and go straight ahead across the next field. Go over a stile on the far side, then after 10 yards turn right through a gate.

3. Turn right on the path, then after another 10 yards turn left on a grassy path, through the woodland. Ignore a path bearing right and keep straight ahead. When you reach a gravel path, bear right to continue in the same direction. Go through a gate with the water to the right and left. Follow the path round to the right, to walk with the water on your right. Where the path divides, keep right to stay by the water. Go through a gate, up the steps and turn right at the top.

There are seats here for a coffee break.

Go ahead on this gravel path. Drop down some steps, go over a stile, then after 10 yards go left through a wooden gate.
4. The path goes up through the woodland and joins a fence on your left. Where the fence ends, bear right to join a path through the trees to reach the access road to Calke Abbey, which is to your left.

A number of active ghosts haunt this imposing building. In the information and ticket office, staff have been slapped or pinched and the wooden chairs have been found on the table. Many members of the public have seen a hooded monk in the toilet block. In the Old Brewhouse, footsteps have been heard to race along the servants' passage and up the stone stairs.

In the former drawing room on the first floor, now a library, an elderly lady thought to be Nanny Pearce has been seen. She stayed on after the children grew up and now her ghost sits and watches visitors.

In the boudoir, a lady in period dress was seen, looking like the portrait in the room, which is that of Lady Caroline, wife of the 5th Baronet. The visitor who saw her assumed she was an actress until he was told there were none in the building that day and realised he had seen a ghost.

5. Turn right. Where the road goes to the right, leave it to go ahead through a wooden gate. Continue on the lane. Go through an iron gate and ahead to reach a wooden gate, leading on to a road. Go straight ahead, then after 20 yards go left at a public footpath sign. Go straight ahead for four fields,

*Calke Abbey is haunted by many ghosts
who may slap or pinch you.*

keeping the fence, hedge or boundary always on your left-hand side, to emerge eventually on to a road.

6. Turn left. Go down the road for 200 yards (ignoring a sign to the right for Ivanhoe Way) to a junction. Bear right here at the sign for Staunton Harold Hall and Ivanhoe Way. Go up the road. When you reach a sign for a 'Hidden Dip!', bear left off the road at a yellow arrow sign, going across the field on a broad path, following the direction of the arrow to reach a high hedge. Continue ahead, with the hedge on your right. Go over a stile and ahead into woodland. Go through a gap stile and follow the direction of the arrow down a hill, over a footbridge, up the steps and to the right. Pass a pond to the left and continue to a second pond to the right.

Your route lies to the left up the steps, but cross the footbridge to the right as it is worth pausing for a moment at this pond, which is the haunt of a kingfisher and is covered in dragonflies. It is called Laundry Pond and was originally a quarry for lime kilns, which are now buried in its depths. There has been limestone quarrying in this area since 1300.

The area is called Dimminsdale, which is thought to be derived from Demon's Dale. However, there do not seem to be any stories to explain this, and it may be that the glow of the fires of the lime kilns looked ghostly and evil in mediaeval times.

The pool is called Laundry Pond because a knoll overlooking the pool is the former site of a cottage, which was the laundry for Staunton Harold Hall.

Return from the pond and go up the steps. Go up the path, over a footbridge and on to a road.

7. Turn right. Go up the road, past another car park for Staunton Harold Reservoir. Go round a right-hand bend, then look for a stile in the left-hand hedge, which has 'Undiscovered ends' carved on it.

See if you can work out what the message is that is given on the far side of each stile. I warn you that you are doing it in reverse!

Go into the wood on Pemissive Path, following the yellow arrow sign bearing right. When you reach a broad track, go left. Turn right at the yellow arrow, through a stile saying 'There's nothing'. Go left over a stile saying 'Worth the wear'. Go right through the stile saying 'Of winning' and the last stile leading on to a road saying 'But laughter.'

8. Cross the road and go ahead over the stile saying 'And the love' and continue on Permissive Path. Go straight down the field then go right and through a kissing gate into woodland. Cross the bridge over the stream then over a stile with 'Of friends' on it.

The two sayings are, therefore: There's nothing worth the wear of winning but laughter and the love of friends. The reverse phrase is: Our pared legs stand (meaning the stile's) to let your paired legs pass. Give us your hand.

Follow the arrow sign into a field, to walk with the hedge on your left, to reach a yellow post in the far corner. Go over a stile with '1994' on it. Bear left, past the yellow-tipped post to the next stile and then across the field and continue with the wood to your left. Where the wood ends, go ahead on a broad cart track. At a second open gateway, where the cart track goes left to the farm, leave it to bear right, following the arrow sign. Go down the hill, over a stile and to the right, walking with the hedge on your right.

The top of Breedon Hill Church may be glimpsed on the horizon to the right.

Continue by the side of Quarry Wood. Leaving the wood behind, cross a stile into a field, going right for 10 yards first, to pick up a clear path across it. Go over the stile and across the following field to a kissing gate on to a lane.

9. Turn left. The water to the left is The Pool at Melbourne. Go along the road until you reach the imposing frontage of Melbourne Hall to your right.

Melbourne Hall, where a ghostly lady sits quietly sewing.

Melbourne Hall was built in 1630 using stones from the ruined Melbourne Castle by Sir John Coke, Secretary of State to Charles I. His descendant, Thomas Coke, laid out the gardens some 60 years later. It is his sister Betty, who was a great beauty in her day, who haunts this hall. She has been seen by visitors in one of the bedrooms working on a tapestry, which she began in her lifetime but left unfinished when she died. Now her ghost returns to sit quietly sewing.

During Queen Victoria's reign, the hall was occupied by William Lamb, Lord Melbourne, who was her Prime Minister. His wife, Lady Caroline Lamb, had a number of scandalous affairs, including one with Lord Byron at nearby Newstead Abbey. Her ghost is said to wander around the gardens and vanish into the arbour known as the birdcage.

Go around a right-hand bend. Your route lies on the second road to the left after the bend, between the church and the war memorial. Turn left here.

The tea rooms, together with craft shops and access to Melbourne Hall gardens, are almost opposite this road.

Go down the road and ahead down a narrow path between the walls, to emerge on to a lane. Turn left on the lane (not right, which leads to the main road). Pass Salsbury Lane on the right, then after 150 yards turn left at a public footpath to Woodhouses through a kissing gate. The path drops down the hill. Where it divides, take the right-hand fork to walk with the hedge on your right. Continue in the same direction in the following field to reach a road.

10. Cross over it and turn left. Pass Robinson's Hill to the right and continue to the next road, where you turn right to Staunton Harold Reservoir on Calke Road. Go up the access road. Pass the first sign displaying the times when the gate closes. At a second sign, where the dam is to the left, leave the road and go into the woodland. Follow the winding path through the trees to reach the car park.

Bibliography

Anthony, Wayne *Haunted Derbyshire* Breedon Books Publishing Co Ltd, 1997.
Armitage, Jill *Haunted Places of Derbyshire* Countryside Books, 2005.
Bell, David *Derbyshire Ghosts and Legends* Countryside Books, 2003.
Daniel, Clarence *Ghosts of Derbyshire* Galava Printing Co Ltd, 1973.
McMeeken, Louis *Peak Place Names* Halsgrove, 2003.

Index